DATE DUE

CONQUER
INTERVIEW
OBJECTIONS

CONQUER INTERVIEW OBJECTIONS

Robert F. Wilson
and
Erik H. Rambusch

JOHN WILEY & SONS, INC.

New York ▪ Chichester ▪ Brisbane ▪ Toronto ▪ Singapore

In recognition of the importance of preserving what has been written, it is a policy of John Wiley & Sons, Inc., to have books of enduring value published in the United States printed on acid-free paper, and we exert our best efforts to that end.

Copyright © 1994 by John Wiley & Sons, Inc.
Published by John Wiley & Sons, Inc.

This publication is designed to provide accurate and authoritative information in regard to the subject matter covered. It is sold with the understanding that the publisher is not engaged in rendering legal, accounting, or other professional services. If legal advice or other expert assistance is required, the services of a competent professional person should be sought. *From a Declaration of Principles jointly adopted by a Committee of the American Bar Association and a Committee of Publishers.*

Library of Congress Cataloging-in-Publication Data:

Wilson, Robert F.
    Conquer interview objections / by Robert F. Wilson and Erik
  H. Rambusch.
       p.   cm.
    Includes index.
    ISBN 0-471-58981-0. — ISBN 0-471-58982-9 (pbk.)
    1. Employment interviewing.   2. Job Hunting.
  I. Rambusch, Erik H., 1941–   II. Title.
  HF5549.5.I6W56   1994
  650.14—dc20   93-29358

Printed in the United States of America

10 9 8 7 6 5 4 3 2 1

Introduction

Most job interviewing advice is reduced to one of two sharply contrasting approaches. On one side of the table are the "Just answer the questions and don't make waves" advisers. On the other are those who insist that the only path to success is to "Show the interviewer that you're in charge."

Limiting interview participation to answering direct questions makes it difficult for an interviewee to address his own agenda. An accomplishment or skill crucial to performing the job may never come up if it is not part of the answer to an interviewer's question. And because it is not dealt with, the interviewee's known qualifications remain incomplete.

There are a couple of problems with the "take charge of the interview" alternative, as well. First, the interviewee is so intent on prosecuting his case aggressively enough to generate a job offer that he forgets he is the interviewer's guest. By interrupting the flow of the interviewer's questioning to pursue his own agenda, he risks being rude or obnoxious, offending the one person who—at that moment—is in a position to help him the most. This approach usually is doomed as well because the interviewee (taking charge at full speed) doesn't hear critical nuances of the position and its requirements. His strategy has dulled his listening capacity.

There is a third approach—more effective than the first two because it treats the interview experience neither as a petition for mercy nor as a confrontation. Instead, it views the job interview as a genuine business meeting between a buyer with real needs (the prospective employer) and a seller with the potential to fill those needs (the job seeker).

Conquer Interview Objections hones in on three critical ingredients of any well planned sales call that spell the difference between Sale and No Sale:

- Identifying the buyer's needs
- Overcoming objections
- Making the close

To a job finder, "identifying the buyer's needs" translates to learning all of the requirements of the job—including unique character traits that may require probing questions to uncover. "Overcoming objections" means recognizing and neutralizing specific soft spots in one's candidacy. "Making the close" becomes asking for the job.

Yet logical as it sounds, these three valuable techniques are rarely employed in the job interview. Why? Because they are perceived as being tactically so chancy—not to mention anxiety-producing—that most interviewees avoid the perceived risk rather than probe for unasked questions that may damage their chances for the job.

Conquer Interview Objections identifies and demystifies these crucial aspects of the job interview and converts them to the powerful, competitive tools so important in a volatile economy. It teaches the job seeker when and how to apply these techniques in an effective, non-threatening manner to create a win-win situation—the best possible climate for a productive job interview benefitting both sides.

For answers to job-search problems that precede the interviewing process, be sure to take a look at our companion book, *Conquer Resume Objections*.

PRONOUN/ADJECTIVE GENDER ALERT

Throughout this book our contribution to controlling the rampant use of "his or her," "his/her," "s/he," and "he/she," as well as various annoying single subject-plural pronoun combinations, has been to generally characterize *job seekers* as male and *interviewers* as female. This is hardly an ideal solution, and to some may be equally annoying. We're open to suggestions.

Acknowledgments

A number of friends and colleagues have contributed to the quality of this manuscript, among them Martha Buchanan, Mike Hamilton, Maureen Drexel, Carmel Bruder, Tom Widney, John Tarrant, Lance Barclay, Charles Bove, Fran Williams, Nancy Jo Geiger, Jack Couch, Blanche Parker, Chuck Wielgus, and Dave Brinkerhoff.

Contents

Appendixes

CONQUER INTERVIEW OBJECTIONS

CONQUER INTERVIEW OBJECTIONS

Rectangles represent steps in the process that must be completed
before proceeding. Diamonds represent decision points.

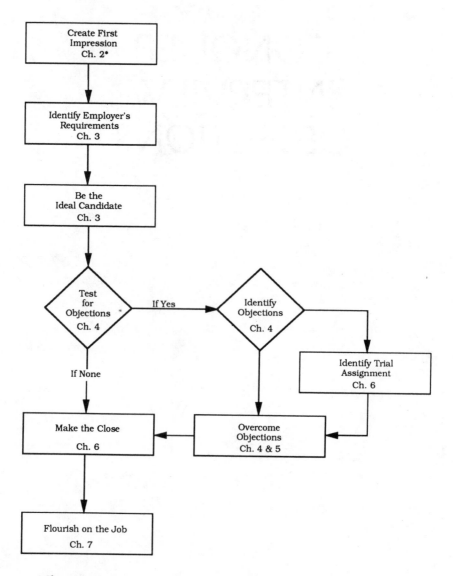

* Chapter 1 consists of an overview of marketing strategy.

1

Research and Reconnaissance

During the late 1980s, management consultant W. Edwards Deming shook up the American workplace with a philosophy he called "continuous quality improvement." Deming and his followers challenged the American notion of individualism for its own sake and proposed putting power in the hands of the workers instead. (Because Deming previously spent 30 years working toward the same end with government and corporate leaders in Japan, this movement is sometimes called the "Japanese school of management.")

For many top-down-run U.S. companies, such a revolutionary notion will take a while to catch on, deeply rooted as existing corporate hierarchies and power bases are. Nevertheless, the signs are real that permanent change is on its way. Teamwork and shared management are examples of Deming's theories that are becoming real alternatives in the workplace.

For purposes of this book, the assumption of empowerment is consistent with the way you will learn to interview. Part of this has to do with your state of mind and attitude as you go through the interviewing process.

Knowing that the individual interviewing you may one day be your boss can affect your performance. Nevertheless, it is a mistake to prematurely assume the position of underdog (employee reporting to employer) to the extent that you fail to ask—and to answer—

the penetrating questions that will help you and the employer decide whether you want each other.

INFORMATION GATHERING

The interviewing process begins with information gathering. Your success in any job interview is almost entirely dependent on the quantity and quality of the research that establishes your strategy for that first meeting. There is no way you can be perceived as the solution to an employer's problem, after all, if you don't take the time to learn what one or more of those problems are—and why they have come to be.

Not long ago the human resources department of a Wall Street area financial newspaper chain—part of a foreign-owned business information corporation—interviewed 25 candidates as part of its search for a circulation director. These 25 men and women were selected from more than 200 respondents to display advertisements placed in publications most likely to be seen by interested candidates.

Although the company was not identified in the ads, there was no question that in the week or two it took to arrange an interview, those contacted about the position could find out as much about it as their investigative skills allowed.

But what happened? The opening question in each interview was: "Before we discuss your background and our needs, would you please tell me what you already know about our current publication and chain of newspapers"?

A composite standard response went like this: "You are well known in the industry—I've heard your name numerous times in my [various sales, circulation, and marketing positions]. And yes, I believe you are owned by a foreign company."

This was the full extent of all 25 candidates' preparation—the *top* candidates' preparation. Not one called the office beforehand to inquire about the company. Even more surprisingly, few if any had used other sources of information to learn something about the organization—even though they expressed interest in being employed there.

Sound preparation for a job interview is good sense for a number of reasons:

- *The more a job candidate knows about a company and the way it works, the more realistically he can project himself as a company problem solver on a permanent, full-time basis.* Learning from customers, vendors, and competitors—as well as from current and former employees about a company's weaknesses and problem areas—adds a dimension of objectivity that information supplied by the company sometimes lacks. Being able to converse knowledgeably about a company's strengths and weaknesses also allows a candidate to be viewed as a professional who thoroughly investigates a situation before acting on it. A prospective employer can more easily visualize the candidate's ability to perform his duties on the job in a consistently effective manner.

- *The more a person knows about a company, the more likely it will be that he is perceived as a problem solver.* Speaking easily and lucidly about such matters as new product-line additions, a current advertising campaign, or recent public statements by company officers permits a candidate to use up-to-date—yet non-proprietary—data in a way that leads to greater rapport with a prospective employer, and thus a better opportunity to deepen the relationship.

- *The more a person knows about a company, the easier it will be to decide whether he wants to work there.* Finding out about relationships between departments, divisions—and, perhaps most importantly, managers and staff—helps to recognize the value a company places on performance and how it rewards employees for exemplary performance.

Interviewing Outside an Industry or Function

If you are changing careers—even slightly—from your current industry or function, planning and positioning become even more important. It also requires extensive repackaging of such written credentials as your resumes and cover letters (topics dealt with more thoroughly in our companion book, *Conquer Resume Objections.*)

You have passed at least the first test in the process simply by getting the interview in the first place. But because you will be seen by some interviewers as an industry or functional alien, your qualifications will be called into question in ways that may surprise you.

For this reason it is essential that you speak with some knowledge of your target company's customers, competitors, and clients, as well as its infrastructure. Extensive interviews with individuals in your new industry or function are a must. Read on for specific suggestions.

MARKET RESEARCH

The following two examples show how market research can make or break a product. First example: Years ago Ford Motor Company launched a new model car without adequately testing the market waters. Management was solidly behind it—they even named it after one of Henry's grandsons. From both engineering and manufacturing standpoints, the Edsel was a fine automobile. But when prospective buyers saw its bizarre front end ("funny looking" to some; plain "ugly" to others), they avoided Ford showrooms in record numbers. It took the company years to recover its financial and credibility losses. It will take longer to eliminate "Edsel" from the industrial lexicon as a synonym for failure.

Second example: Procter & Gamble spent more than a year to learn that many customers wanted to buy whole, unbroken potato chips—no potato chip parts, no crumbs, just whole chips. Enter Pringles, the processed potato chip stacked in a can (last chip same as the first), every chip whole until eaten. Since the first successful Pringle can was emptied, other market segments have opened doors for Sour Cream and Onion Pringles, Barbecued Pringles, "Lite" Pringles, and Rippled Pringles.

The key difference in these two stories is that Procter & Gamble accurately identified and isolated a consumer desire (for an "unbroken chip"), and delivered on it. Ford, on the other hand, *assumed* its Edsel would be successful because the car was soundly engineered. Unfortunately, it didn't conduct sufficient market research to validate the assumption.

Similarly, your market research must ferret out prospective employers' needs, which in turn will allow you to present yourself as the ideal candidate to fulfill them.

A number of the research sources introduced in Chapter 4 of *Conquer Interview Objections* will be helpful to you in generating more information on companies with which you have arranged interviews. These sources will be summarized here for easy reference.

General Interest and Industry-Specific Directories

Dozens of regional, national, and international business directories are available in most public libraries. They contain the information you need—not only for publicly held companies, but for private firms as well. Some of these directories are classified by industry, others by size of company. A selection of both general reference and industry-specific directories is given at the end of the chapter. If you don't see your specialty listed, ask a local public or university librarian for assistance. Try also the *Directories in Print* (formerly *Directory of Directories*), a research timesaver that will lead you to the directories of most possible assistance to you.

One of the best of the general directories is *The Directory of Corporate Affiliations*, published annually (with bimonthly supplements), by the National Register Publishing Company. A front-of-the-book index lists more than 5,000 parent companies—in boldface, to distinguish them (in user-friendly fashion) from their 57,000 respective divisions, subsidiaries, and affiliates. For each of these you'll find an address, phone number, business description, stock exchange ticker symbol, annual sales, number of employees, and names of top corporate officers. Additional geographical and Standard Industrial Code (S.I.C.) indexes list all companies by city and state, and primary types of business. Another back-of-the-book feature is an index of "corporate responsibility"—a way to find in one place all of the human resource directors, CEOs, treasurers, and purchasing agents, among others. Five annual supplements document significant corporate changes, including acquisitions, mergers, and other dramatic name or status switches.

Additional DOCA volumes provide similar information for 8,000 U.S. private companies and 33,000 international companies.

Other Library Sources

Check out the special issues of leading business magazines and trade journals for annually updated marketing, sales, and product development information. Also, ask about recent computer software that call out references to national companies in business and consumer magazines. One worth looking for is ProQuest, available in many public libraries. (A complete list of general interest and industry-specific sources appears at the end of the chapter.)

The Target Company as Source

Another good way to gather intelligence about the company for which you're interviewing is from its most recent annual report, 10–K (for a more detailed look at the company financials), or any descriptive literature available from its marketing or public relations departments. These publications offer a full range of information about a company's products and services, including recent projections of long-range strategies and objectives. Annual reports and 10–Ks will give you a better notion of a company's financial status and growth strategy. Call the company and tell the operator what you want. She'll connect you with the appropriate department.

Maximizing Opportunities

Though this book focuses on your performance in job interviews already scheduled, the reality is that you must continue to generate leads at target companies you haven't yet penetrated. The tendency is to let up a little on your job search efforts after you line up one or two interviews. If you do, though, and the expected job offer does not materialize for one reason or another, your pipeline is empty. Weeks could go by before you are able to set up initial interviews at new target companies, with a concomitant erosion of your precious cash reserves—not to mention confidence and morale.

To keep this from happening, treat even the most promising job opportunity as just that—an opportunity, which may or may not lead to a job offer. Such healthy skepticism will keep you more realistic about your job search as a whole, and motivate you to spend more energy on early steps in the process: identifying and contacting companies on your "A" list, until you exhaust it and prepare another list to replace it.

FOUR AVENUES TO MARKET

Most surveys rate the four most common ways, in terms of effectiveness, to reach target companies as follows:

1. Networking (overwhelmingly)
2. Executive recruitment and employment agencies
3. Print advertising
4. Direct mail

Here is a brief summary of each of these methods, as a reminder that you need to concentrate on these early stages of the job search as hard as you do to prepare for an interview.

Networking

The most effective conventional job-search marketing strategy is networking—now standard practice, even a buzzword, among job seekers and job-search counselors. Reduced to its essentials, the concept of networking is that your chances of finding a job improve in direct proportion to the number of influential people you meet in companies that have—or may have—job openings, or who know of other companies where this might be so. Often this is a two- or three-step process, but it works.

Just think why networking improves your chances to a much greater extent than do other methods. From the employer's point of view the hiring process becomes a dream: There are no fees to recruiters or employment agencies; no advertising costs; no need to pore through hundreds of resumes. It's just you and your prospective employer, one on one, no strings attached.

When a viable candidate materializes between the time a need has been identified and the specs have been written, after all, there is no need to advertise. Granted, your timing must be virtually perfect to snag the opening just forming. On the other hand, the time frame also allows you to audition for similar jobs that might be available—without the competition from hundreds of other qualified individuals. This is a luxury applicants from the other three avenues to market never have.

This body of available and about-to-be-available positions is often called "the hidden job market." Many of the jobs are filled quickly by those tapped into the networks mentioned here (and in more detail in Chapter 4 of *Conquer Resume Objections*). They are "hidden" only to job seekers who don't work hard and don't do their homework. The trick is for you to become one of these candidates.

Setting Up Your Network

In our networking workshops we encourage people to seek out as many kinds of source groups as they can to broaden the base. Generating raw leads it the first step. If this is a new activity for you, start close to home and fan outward. In each category, develop 15 or more leads that you can subsequently classify and qualify. Use a single sheet of paper for each category. Your long-range interests will be served only if you identify and contact at least 15 individuals in every category. Here is a core list of contact sources; perhaps you can think of others:

1. Husband or wife
2. Relatives
3. Neighbors and community contacts
4. Others who are looking for jobs
5. Professional and trade acquaintances
6. Customers and clients
7. Service people (vendors and suppliers)
8. Former colleagues at previous employers
9. Graduate school, college, or high school classmates
10. Acquaintances through avocations or interests
11. Acquaintances through religious affiliations
12. Former clients or customers

Accomplishing Network Objectives

You have at least three objectives in setting up and conducting your network interviews:

1. To broaden the information base about your target companies, or about competitors that may become target companies

2. To make an ally of your source, to assure a continuing information base
3. To get the names of additional source people at your target companies, or in your function or industry

Overcoming Network Call Objections

We say setting up *and* conducting the network interview, because there may be instances where your source may not agree to see you. If you are persistent (but not a pest), however, you may still extract enough information to make the call worthwhile.

This takes a lot of practice. Early on, your tendency will be to say "Thanks anyway" if you get turned down for a meeting and end it there. As your technique improves, however, you'll learn to use your time more productively—whether in a face-to-face interview or on the phone.

When making a networking call, don't mention that you are looking for a job until you have to and never ask for a job directly. This changes the purpose of the call, as well as your relationship with the source.

It is unlikely that your party knows of a specific job that would interest you. Having to tell you so will likely cause her embarrassment about her inability to help, and she'll look for a quick way to end the call. Result: no additional information, no names of other people to contact, no job possibility, and no likelihood of another conversation at a later date.

When your objective is to uncover information about a particular organization, however, or names of *other* people who might be able to help with your search, your source will be more likely to try to come up with an idea or two. If you've ever been contacted by an executive recruiter, you may recall being asked if you know of anyone qualified or interested in the position under consideration. Networking in this way is one of a recruiter's most effective ways of trolling for candidates.

In trying to reach your contact for the first time you may run into resistance from a secretary. Most are trained to be excellent gatekeepers, and are inclined to give cold callers a hard time. Be polite but persistent and try to make an ally rather than become an adversary. Don't hide the motive for your call or the secretary will be inclined to be even more protective. Practice an introduction that tells the story and imparts a sense of urgency—but not panic. If all else fails, offer to write your contact first if you think pursuing this lead is worth your time.

Specific Network Questions

There are many levels of information useful to you, from identifying a prospective boss to validating the rumor of a new product line that would create jobs *in your specialty,* either now or in the near future. Ask questions that will help you extract as much information of value to you as you can. (Some answers will depend on the level of trust or confidence you've been able to establish with your source):

"What are the possibilities of a merger or acquisition?"

or,

"Is expansion likely . . . the addition of one or more product or service lines?"

or,

"Are sales up (and likely to stay there)?"

or,

"Are any new activities scheduled (probe to see if they may require someone with your capabilities)?"

or,

"Is the company experiencing any particular problems (that a person with your background could help solve)?"

With every information interview, your portfolio of target companies will change. Intelligence of various kinds will cause you to drop some companies, add others, and escalate your level of interest in still others. Keep up-to-date records of your networking interviews together with information about all of the companies on your "A" list, to give you a complete file for job interviews as they develop.

Executive Recruiters and Employment Agencies

Narrow your active list of recruiting firms down to 20 or so, concentrating on those that handle your specialty. (Use *The Directory of Executive Recruiters*, which lists both retainer and contingency recruiters. If you can't find it in your public library write Kennedy Publications, Templeton Road, Fitzwilliam, NH, 03447, or call 1-800-531-0007. Ask for the "Job-Seeker Edition," which lists 2,200 search firms indexed by function, industry, and location. The cost is $39.95. Entries indicate whether a firm will accept unsolicited resumes, but not, unfortunately, how effective it is.

Include a few search firms close enough for you to call on, as well. Occasionally you'll be able to start a relationship with a recruiter willing to exert extra effort on your behalf. This could include tips on your résumé, general job availability climate in your field and function, and (though rarely) the names of other companies in your area that may be hiring (and at which she has not yet been able to land an assignment).

Marketing Tactics With a Recruiter

Start with a phone call, both to permit a personal introduction and to practice your marketing skills. Ask the receptionist to speak with someone in your specialty, by both industry and function. That way, you'll have coverage on two fronts.

If there is no activity in your specialty, waste no more of your time; go on to the next firm. If you get through to the right person, present your case clearly and succinctly, and work for an interview just as you would with a targeted employer. The reason is that you want to make a positive impression on this recruiter—not just for positions she may be working on right now, but for those that may come up in the next several months. (Complete initial marketing strategy for working with executive recruiters can be found in Chapter 4 of *Conquer Resume Objections*.)

Researching a company at which you've set up an interview is much easier if you're working with an executive recruiter or an employment agency. Good ones will help you with the entire interviewing process. Actually, because recruiters make a living from the client fees generated by the candidates they place (never work with a recruiter who charges *you* a fee), it is in their best interest for their candidates to know as much as possible about any assignment they are working on.

As in every other profession, however, some recruiters and agencies are better than others. Since this is the case, here are some data of vital interest to you in performing at your peak efficiency at the interview—as well as helping you decide whether this is a company you want to work for (as adapted from a career transition program called *Job-Bridge*). What the recruiter or agency can't tell you, try to find out on your own:

About the company

- Sales volume for the past two years
  (Consistently up? why?; consistently down? why?; sharp change? why?)
- Profits for the past two years
  (Good sales record with poor profit picture could mean trouble, or could mean possible expansion plans; probe)
- Market share *vis-à-vis* major competitors
  (If not going up, find out why)
- Number of employees for the past two years
  (Static growth or a decrease may indicate problems—including possible downsizing)
- Growth prospects
  (Recent acquisitions or new product lines?)
- Possible problems
  (Why do they exist and how might they be overcome?)

About the position

- Why is it open?
  (If it's a new position, or the previous holder was promoted from it, good; if a termination is involved, be sure it wasn't for a reason that could bring you to the same fate)
- How long has it been open?
  (If two months or more, why is it so difficult to fill?)

- Under what circumstances did the individual leave who previously held the position?
  (Can I talk to him?)
- How many people have been interviewed so far?
  (Why so many—or so few? What has been wrong with them?)
- How many candidates are still in the running?
  (Why are they still being considered?)
- What are the prospects for advancement?
  (If limited, what are the trade-offs?)
- What do you think will be the determining factor in the decision to hire?
  (On what areas should I concentrate my preparation time?)
- Why do you think I would be a good candidate?
  (On what areas should I concentrate in the interview?)
- How many others in the company are doing the same work?
  (What is the likely competition for advancement?
- What is the salary policy? How are raises and promotions determined? How good is the benefits program?
  (Is this an employee-oriented company?)
- How is performance measured?
  (Can I stay motivated here?)

About the boss
- Title?
- Company background? Previous experience?
  (Any common threads?)
- How long with the company? Growth record?
  (Will she take me to the next level or higher?)
- What are her prospects with the company?
  (Same question)
- Management style?
  (Consistent with the way I like to work and can work well?)

- Have you spoken with her personally, or have your conversations been just with personnel?

  (If the former: What are your personal impressions of this person? What do you think the chemistry will be between us?[1]

Such information is crucial in helping you prepare a line of questioning for your interviewer that will both (1) demonstrate your level of preparation, and (2) give you a sense of some real strengths and weaknesses in the company. The second point is one you will want to develop more fully, because it can lead to a realization that this is the job of a lifetime—or one about which you should be extremely skeptical. (You may pick up some of this information in the *Reconnaissance Interview* section introduced on page 15.)

Employment Agencies

Except for a few multioffice firms with functional specialities (Robert Half, in accounting, for example) most employment agencies work a relatively small territory, rarely transcending a metropolitan area. You can get a pretty good idea of their effectiveness by the number of ads they run locally, and of their ethical standing by checking with the Better Business Bureau. As a general rule, employment agency counselors are less sophisticated in the ways of corporate relationships and infrastructure than their search counterparts. They usually do know their business locally, however, and can be good source people if you establish a good relationship and don't become a pest.

Newspaper and Magazine Advertisements

Job offers through classified advertising are a long shot, but obviously they work to some degree because so many hiring companies and employment agencies continue to use them. The thing is, most job seekers think the classifieds are the only marketing source. That's what drives the odds so high.

For this reason, pick your spots carefully, There could be hundreds—even thousands—of other respondents. Answer only those

---

[1]*Job-Bridge.* © Wilson McLeran, Inc., New Haven, CT 06511.

ads for which your qualifications are a perfect match. If five qualifications are listed, you should have four of them without a stretch.
If this is so, you have three remaining tasks:

1. Rework those parts of your resume that will allow you to
   make a stronger case as the ideal candidate. Add to your
   Summary, for example, any aspects of your background
   that match the job's requirements. This will make it easier
   on a first reader trying to visualize you in the job.

2. Thoroughly research the company to ascertain the reasons
   for the opening and any additional information that will
   allow you to write a cover letter specifically positioning you
   for the job. (If you're working from a blind ad, move on to
   point three.) Your letter should state your qualifications for
   the job in the precise sequence the job specs are listed in
   the ad.

3. Wait at least a week before sending off your response to a
   newly listed job. Early responses tend to get lost in the ava-
   lanche of others. Later letters are read more thoroughly because there are fewer of them. For examples of good cover
   letters, see Appendix B and Chapters 3 and 4 of *Conquer
   Resume Objections*.

Direct Mail

The broadcast letter, a job-search variation of the shotgun approach,
is the primary application of direct mail. Because such a large
volume of resumes must be generated to make a mass mailing even
minimally effective, there is no way to personalize your approach.
This, in essence, reduces your candidacy to that of the lowest
common denominator—hardly likely to make you stand out from
the thousands of others using the same approach. For an example
of a good one, if you decide to use direct mail, see Appendix B.

RECONNOITERING YOUR TARGET COMPANY

For the most part, *Conquer Interview Objections* will discuss hiring
interviews—and to a lesser extent screening interviews. There are

two other types of job interviews, though, that are key to a successful search. One is the networking interview, covered earlier in this chapter (and more thoroughly in Chapter 4 of *Conquer Resume Objections*). The other form of interview actually is an assertive form of research called the reconnaissance interview, borrowed from an exploratory military survey of enemy territory of the same name.

Sometimes the only way to get sufficient information about a job and company in which you're interested and have arranged an interview is to take an inside route. If you have sufficient time before your scheduled screening interview with the company, use the following methods to identify someone with the information to help you learn more:

- Ask your friends, family, colleagues, and acquaintances if they know anybody who works for the target company, or if they know any vendors, competitors, or customers of the company who might have contacts there.
- Check any available directories (alumni, industry, church, etc.) for the names of key employees from the target company or companies with a possible close association to it.
- If you identify more than one contact, call to arrange a visit with as many of them as time permits. The more perspectives you can surface, the better rounded will be the information base you bring to your interview. Your objective will be a personal meeting, which is usually more effective than a phone interview. If the individual you reach is unable or unwilling to meet with you, attempt to get as much information as you can on the phone.

An initial call might go something like those that follow for various kinds of contacts.

With a Current Employee

When your contact is a current employee, assume that word of your call will get back to the individual you are calling about. Ask only for information that is non-proprietary, and maintain a highly professional demeanor that will establish your call as both ethical and appropriate. For example:

"Hello, Mr. Jaeger? This is Al Bachunas. I got your name from Jim Clark, who I understand is a former co-worker of yours. I have an interview a week from Wednesday with Otto Hollerauer, your Director of Purchasing, to talk about an opening in his department.

"Jim tells me you've been in charge of marketing at Universal for the past three years, and I was wondering if you had a few minutes to talk with me about the new compressor product line I've been hearing so much about."

If you get a favorable response, set a time and date. If your source is reluctant to meet with you, attempt to get the information you need before he hangs up, and any other information of value to you that you haven't been able to find elsewhere. See the list of questions under the "Executive Search or Employment Agency Job Orders" section on page 12 for possible questions to which you would like answers. When you've gone as far as you can, a final open-ended probe, such as "Is there anything else you think I ought to know?" either about the company or about the job is sometimes fruitful.

Be careful to ask your questions carefully and honestly, so as to be perceived as neither a pest nor a competitor seeking proprietary information. After all, if your source knows Otto Hollerauer at all he will likely be calling him as soon as he hangs up with you, both to report your call and perhaps to volunteer his impressions of you as a potential employee. (With this in mind, it is also important to mention your conversation with Mr. Jaeger when you meet with Mr. Hollerauer to eliminate the chance of a hidden agenda between you and your prospective boss.)

If your contact is a friend, or perhaps the friend of a friend with whom you feel comfortable, your questions can be somewhat more penetrating. For example:

"What is your job at APS?"

"What is your boss like? Is she typical of the bosses there?"

"Is there a consistent management style at APS? How would you define it?"

"What are your colleagues like? What is the turnover at APS? Does it seem to be static? Going up? Going down?"

"Does management supply you with everything you need to do a good job?"

"Do you receive useful and sufficient feedback regarding your work?"

"Are you fairly compensated? How is good performance rewarded?"

Former Employee

When your contact is a *former* employee (or a vendor or competitor), of course, you need not be quite as diplomatic with your questioning. You may, in fact, be able to exploit a bad relationship between a company and an ex-employee to pick up information you had no idea would be offered you. If things seem to be going well, for example, here are a few followup questions that could yield valuable information about the company:

"What did you like best about working there? What did you like least?"

"In what areas is there the most need for change?"

"Are you aware of any plans to downsize, or to spin off any of their businesses? Are there plans to move any parts of the business elsewhere in the country? Overseas?"

"Why did you leave? Would you work for them again?"

Former Direct Report to Prospective Boss

Even more specific information is available if you are lucky enough to talk with someone who held a position reporting to the individual with whom you are interviewing. Here are a few possibilities:

". . . I understand you worked for Otto Hollerauer at American Products & Services. Well, I have an interview with Mr. Hollerauer next Thursday, and wondered if you had a few minutes to tell me a little bit about the company and, more specifically, what it was like for you to work for him. For example, . . ."

"Can you describe Otto's management style? Did he give you a clear idea of what he expected from you?"

"Did he give you guidelines so you knew if you were on or off course? Can you give me examples?"

"Did he provide regular and thorough feedback regarding your performance to facilitate improvement?"

"How did your colleagues like working for him?"

"As far as you were concerned, what were the most desirable features of working for him? The least desirable?"

"Has your professional development been advanced or hindered working for him? Please explain."

The following three sections indicate the way your conversation might go if your contact is either a competitor, a customer, or a vendor.

Competitor

"Hello, Mr. Shewalter. This is Al Bachunas. A mutual friend, Jim Clark, suggested I call regarding developments in the instrumentation industry. I've heard a lot about American Products & Services lately, and Jim mentioned that you worked for one of their direct competitors. I was wondering what you could tell me about APS, from your perspective."

Here are some followup questions, depending on the responses you get:

"Is APS seen as a tough competitor? Why?"

"What do investors (or other knowledgeable outsiders) see as APS's strengths? What do they see as its soft spots?"

"What products/services are seen as their most profitable? Why is this so? Which are their weakest offerings? Why?"

"Is APS considered a good place to work? Why?"

"Would you consider working for them? Why (or why not)?"

Vendor

". . . I understand you supply parts (or services) to APS."

Followup questions:

"How long have you been working with them?"

"Do they pay their bills on time?"

"Are their specifications clear and consistent?"

"How would you describe their decision-making process from your point of view? (Is it timely, for example, or do most decisions pass through inordinate layers of management before they are finalized?)"

"Are any of APS's competitors among your customers? How

would you compare their effectiveness (or work habits or quality of communication) with that of APS?"

"What do you believe are APS's relative strengths and weaknesses *vis à vis* their competitors?"

Customer

". . . I understand you buy your support services from APS."
Followup questions:
"How long have you been dealing with APS?"
"Why did you choose them? Did you consider (mention names of leading competitors?)"
"Have you ever thought of changing suppliers? Why? Why did you ultimately decide to stay with APS?"
"What do you know about APS as a place to work?"
"Is their billing consistently accurate?" If not . . . "What have been some of the problems? How have they been resolved? What can you tell me about their collection policies and procedures?"
"Have you ever had any other problems with APS? How were they resolved?"

Wrapup

Most of the above questions are open-ended, for an obvious reason: They can't be answered with one word, and so help to keep a discussion moving. They also are non-directive—a respondent is not biased to answer either positively or negatively, and often offers more information than was asked for.

Get in the habit of using open-ended, non-directive questions. They encourage people to be at ease, and produce useful information. People in general enjoy being listened to. The more seriously you listen to them, the more interesting the information they will share with you. Extrapolate this bit of advice to the interview situation—any interview situation—and your chances for success increase exponentially. The more comfortable you are with this technique, the more effectively you will handle open-ended, non-directive questions—particularly when an interviewer uses them on you. This technique is key to becoming an effective interviewee in the various stages of the process in the remaining chapters of *Overcoming Interview Objections.*

GENERAL INTEREST AND INDUSTRY-SPECIFIC LIBRARY SOURCES

Business Organizations, Agencies, and Publications Directory

Business Periodicals Index (350 industries and functions listed)

Corporate 1000

Directory of Corporate Affiliations (U.S. Public Companies; U.S. Private Companies; International Public and Private Companies)

Directory of Directories

Dun's Business Identification (fiche)

Dun's Employment Opportunities Directory

Dun's Million Dollar Directory (Volumes I, II, and III)

Dun's Regional Business Directory

Encyclopedia of Associations

Encyclopedia of Business Information Sources

International Corporate 1000

Macmillan Directory of Leading Private Companies

Small Business Sourcebook

Standard & Poor (Industry Surveys; Corporation Listings; Directory of Company Officers)

Standard Directory of Advertisers

Thomas Register

World Business Directory

INDUSTRY-SPECIFIC DIRECTORIES

American Architects' Directory

American Hospital Association Guide to the Health Care Field

American Library Directory
Automotive News Market Data Book
Chemical Engineering Catalog
Commercial Real Estate Brokers Directory
Conservation Yearbook
Corporate Finance Bluebook
Design News
Directory of the Computer Industry
Directory of Management Consultants
Dun & Bradstreet Reference Book of Transportation
Dun's Industrial Guide: The Metalworking Directory
Editor and Publisher Market Guide
Electrical/Electronic Directory
Electronic Design's Gold Book
Fairchild's Textile and Apparel Financial Directory
International Petroleum Register
Kline Guide to the Paper & Pulp Industry
Literary Market Place: The Directory of American Book Pub-
   lishing
Magazine Industry Market Place
Moody's Manuals (for various industries)
O'Dwyer's Directory of Corporate Communications
O'Dwyer's Directory of Public Relations Agencies
Polk's World Bank Directory
Printing Trades Blue Book
Progressive Grocer's Marketing Guidebook
Standard & Poor's Security Dealers of North America
Standard Directory of Advertising Agencies
Telephony's Directory of the Telephone Industry
The Uncle Sam Connection, a Guide to Federal Employment
Thomas Register of American Manufacturers
Whole World Oil Directory
Who's Who in Advertising

Who's Who in Electronics
Who's Who in Insurance
Who's Who in Water Supply and Pollution Control
World Airline Record

ON COMPUTER

Infotrac (journal and newspaper index)

Business Dateline OnDisc (business articles in local, state and regional journals, and newspapers)

ProQuest (business articles in newspapers and magazines)

Standard & Poor's Corporations (public and private companies and biographical listings)

Ultimate Job Finder (4,500 sources of trade and specialty journals)

ADDITIONAL READING

Bridges, William. *Making Sense of Life's Transitions: Strategies for Coping With the Difficult, Painful, and Confusing Times in Your Life.* Reading, MA: Addison-Wesley, 1980. Step-by-step through the transition process, offering skills and suggestions for negotiating life's transitions.

Covey, Stephen, R. *Principle-Centered Leadership.* New York: Simon & Schuster, 1991. How to maintain a sense of stability and security in a culture characterized by change, flexibility, and a demand for continuous improvement.

Katzenbach, Jon R., and Douglas K. Smith. *The Wisdom of Teams: Creating the High Performance Organization.* Boston: Harvard Business School Press, 1992. Clear, fresh approach to an idea most managers think they already understand. Combines theory with case presentations.

2

The First Impression

Forget what you've heard about first impressions. Most Americans who work for a living will have plenty of opportunities to make a good one—even in a job interview. Given the rate at which Americans change jobs in a lifetime (currently once every six years), this is a skill that should easily be acquirable over time.

Still, it is true: A single, bad first impression can kill your chances for a job, even in a preliminary interview with a functionary screening interviewer.

No matter how magnificent your qualifications, an interviewer can decide almost immediately that you just won't do. The judgment against you may have nothing to do with your ability to do the job, but still be completely beyond your control. Here are some of the most frequent reasons your first impression could knock you out of contention, followed by suggestions for recognizing the situation and taking remedial action for the next opportunity:

Misreading the Interviewer

- You neglected to adjust your approach based on your perception of the interviewer's personality and priorities.

Physical appearance

- You violated one or more of the norms of basic business dress, neatness, or hygiene.

Body language and mannerisms

- Your interview manner conveyed—accurately or inaccurately—fear, discomfort, arrogance, or superiority.

Vocabulary and diction

- You betrayed, through your word choice or enunciation, a manner of speaking jarring to your interviewer for whatever reason.

Preparedness

- Your unreadiness for the interview manifested itself in a lack of confidence or professionalism.

Poor or badly disciplined listening skills

- While questions were being asked, you concentrated more on answers you would give than to the specifics of the questions themselves.
- You failed to pick up nuances or hidden meanings in your interviewer's questions.
- You heard "what you wanted to hear" and answered questions that were not asked, either wholly or in part.

MISREADING THE INTERVIEWER

Your best first impression has much to do with whether your interviewer can visualize you as a functioning "member of the team." This extremely subjective judgment—part of the definition of "personal chemistry"—is often formed very early in the meeting, often in the first 30 seconds.

The fact that the impression is subjective, though, does not mean that you are powerless to influence it. Just understand that your power is manifest in direct proportion to your ability to understand and identify with the interviewer's motives. Those motives, in turn, are affected at least partially by the interviewer's personality. If your reconnaissance interviews have yielded significant information about your interviewer, you will be that much further ahead.

This is a topic difficult to describe without appearing to give it more weight than is due. When you go into any interview, after all, you have a lot on your mind. It is difficult to internalize an additional responsibility that could adversely affect your level of concentration on other matters you believe to be more important.

Even so, being able to "read" your interviewer instantly may give you the edge you need over your competitors for the job. If your powers of observation help you lock onto your interviewer's goals (as well as find out how she sets them), you'll find it much easier to assure a good first impression.

One of the quickest ways to get a fix on the intellectual and emotional factors that drive an interviewer's decision-making is to determine the dominant personality type at work which, in turn, is based on two criteria:

1. Emotional, unconscious and/or psychodynamic factors

2. Logical, conscious and/or rational factors

Let's call group number one the "Heart Factors" and group number two the "Head Factors." Each person's mix of Head and Heart is unique; the odds are highly unlikely that any individual personality will fall solely within one of the four general personality types (see the Figure on p. 24). Nearly all of us are a mix of the four, in virtually infinite combinations. So don't pay attention to the labels within the boxes. These are pure forms, infrequently represented in real life.

All of this said, it is still crucial to get a handle on your interviewer. An accurate Head and Heart reading is an effective quick study, allowing you to adapt your tactics as necessary. So review the Figure on page 28 and see what you can learn from it.

Let's arrange the above sets of criteria on two scales to delineate the four general personality types (represented by the figure on p. 28). Then explore the tactics you can use to communicate most effectively with whatever permutation of each you run up against. Horizontally, we'll align the Heart issues from left to right, low to high. Vertically, we'll align the Head issues from bottom to top, low to high.

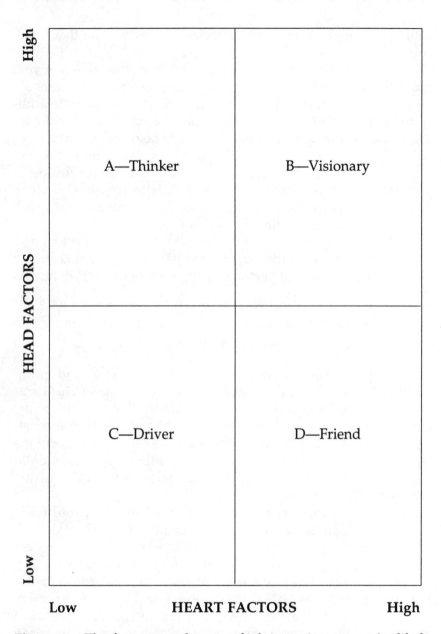

Figure 1. The four general types of job interviewers you're likely to meet are loosely identified in the quadrants shown above. These are generalizations representing *tendencies*, remember, and do not describe actual people.

Four Interviewer Personality Types

It is time to take a closer look at the interviewing approaches of the four interviewer personality types.

The Thinker

This personality type will make decisions about you primarily on the basis of head facts with very little on heart. Given the opportunity, she will have studied your resume thoroughly before meeting you and will use it as a guide during the interview. She will spend considerable time on any apparent discrepancies between resume entries and points made by you during the interview. She will want to hear details of who, what, and why regarding major events in your career. She will probably take notes, reveal few emotions, and make small talk awkwardly, if at all. She will move the interview along in a logical, fast-paced way, zeroing in on any perceived benchmark career responsibilities and accomplishments. She will want all of the details regarding key events, such as who reported to whom, budgetary concerns, if any, and actions and decisions for which you were specifically responsible.

Here are some adjectives that describe most Thinkers:

- Logical
- Deliberate
- Objective
- Detailed
- Analytical
- Sequential
- Precise

The Driver

The Driver combines both head and heart factors in reaching a conclusion, but only to a modest degree. Her office will be neat and furnished in bold colors with strong, heavy materials. The interview will start on time because she values her schedule. Like the thinker, she wants facts—not drily retold as in a computer printout, but in war-story fashion so she can savor the details.

Many drivers demand total control and loyalty; they look first for subordinates who will supplement their fiefdoms. For this reason they screen out most candidates showing a lot of individual initiative. If working on a short leash is not your style, you may well save yourself an unhappy job experience by flunking the Driver's test.

Here are some adjectives that describe most Drivers:

- Results-oriented
- Assertive
- Technically skilled
- Practical
- Functional
- Decisive
- Compulsive

The Visionary

This personality type bases her hiring decisions on much more than precisely worded job descriptions. Her own Head and Heart readings can vary widely, but both usually tend toward the high side. She is more interested in the big picture and in long-range applications of policy and procedures than she is in immediate, day-to-day implementation. How candidates might fit into organizational structure is not the Visionary's primary concern. How they might be able to apply current experience to future problems, however, is. Don't look for a conventional line of questioning from a Visionary. Expect instead some seemingly off-the-wall questions, perhaps based on hypothetical premises, as she tries to visualize you in a number of different kinds of situations and relationships.

Here are some adjectives that describe most Visionaries:

- Original
- Imaginative
- Creative
- Broad-gauged
- Charismatic
- Idealistic

- Intellectually tenacious
- Ideological

The Friend

This interviewer is likely to make her decision on the basis of her professional comfort level, or "gut feel." She will depend more on Heart issues and less on Head issues. Look around her office and you'll see pictures of family and business friends, and maybe a company golf trophy. The Friend will try to make you feel comfortable, and find common interest areas to put you both at ease. She may offer you a cup of coffee (saying yes will start the bonding process), and start the interview with some comments about the weather or the ease with which you found the office. Answer all of her questions fully and factually, but in as friendly a way as they were asked in order to keep the rapport at a high level.

Here are some adjectives that describe most Friends:

- Spontaneous
- Persuasive
- Empathic
- Values-oriented
- Probing
- Introspective
- Loyal

Never feel that adjusting your presentation and responses to the interviewer's personality is an act of dishonesty. You are not pretending to be someone other than yourself, after all, only to be exposed as a fraud once you are on the payroll. You are simply adapting your presentation to the needs and priorities you sense your interviewer has.

All of us behave differently in different situations, after all: When we are with family and friends we act one way; when we meet strangers we behave another. Many of us even act differently with some members of our family—as well as with some friends— than we do with others. Our societal norms have taught us that such differentiation of behaviors facilitates communication.

Keep in mind that "persona," the Latin word for "person," goes back to the masks Roman actors wore in portraying different characters on stage. (See Appendix A to see how the first few minutes of an interview might go with each of the four personality types described above, and Appendix E of *Conquer Resume Objections* to apply the four types to your own managerial tendencies.)

PHYSICAL APPEARANCE

Military metaphor: A sergeant needs six "volunteers" for morning latrine and kitchen duty. The recruits who routinely escape such assignments are often those who can rely on a knack for virtual invisibility while in formation. Those more easily identified—with wrinkled shirts, dull brass, cockeyed caps, or whatever—are usually available in sufficient quantities to fill out any duty roster.

What's the point? *Don't draw attention to yourself in any way that distracts the interviewer from your message.*

For the most part, passing the interview physical appearance test is largely a matter of exercising common sense. Those found wanting in any aspect of this relatively superficial, often subtle, but nevertheless seriously considered criterion will be assumed deficient in other matters as well, and almost certainly will be passed over. Here are three commonly abused areas.

Basic Business Dress

Part of the definition of common sense as it applies to this section has to do with keeping up with the times. Make it your business, if you don't already know, to learn what appropriate dress means in your locale, at your level, and in your industry. A corporate opening in New York, Chicago, or Los Angeles, for example, whether for mailroom assistant or chief financial officer, may mean adhering to a higher level of formality, sophistication, or awareness of style than would apply in less fashion-conscious parts of the country.

Spend some time observing appropriate dress for your particular situation (by locale, level, and industry) to ensure your ability to make the right decisions when the time comes. Keep in mind that a fashion statement is not your primary objective (exceptions noted below). Dressing somewhat more conservatively than you believe necessary, then, is not a bad idea.

If your taste in clothes is marginal or worse, ask someone better at it than you to help put together one or two interview outfits. Be prepared to make a sizable investment, and avoid polyester shortcuts that may save a few bucks but lose you the job offer.

Men should wear a dark, solid-color or pinstriped suit. Wear a white shirt to be safe, with solid-color or small patterned tie and dark, solid-colored socks. The industry or function in which you are interviewing may affect your decision somewhat. In the advertising, public relations, fashion, and other corollary industries, for example, the tendency is toward a slightly more flamboyant look. Find out for yourself before you select your outfit.

For a woman, a conservative theme also applies, with the exceptions noted above. A well-tailored suit, contrasting skirt and jacket, or a fashionable street dress are appropriate. Apply makeup and perfume modestly and avoid noisy jewelry altogether.

The thing is, you want nothing so superficial as a jangling bracelet or a loud tie to dilute your ultimate message: You can do the job effectively, as well as fit in smoothly with your future coworkers.

Neatness

Sure neatness counts. It counts a lot more with some prospective employers than with others, of course, but either way, don't allow a hiring decision to be based on such a frivolous lack of attention to detail.

These are all obvious considerations anyway: shined shoes, cleaned and pressed clothes, combed hair, cleanly shaven, cleaned and buffed nails. Be sure to arrive at your destination five minutes early, to allow yourself time for a restroom check to correct what wind or weather might have put askew.

Hygiene

Leave nothing to chance; take time enough to shower in the morning rather than the night before. Use whatever deodorant/antiperspirant you are sure will keep you both dry and odor-free. Use mouthwash if bad breath has been a problem for you in the past. If you have a head or chest cold not severe enough to cause you to postpone your meeting, be certain you can control any coughing or sneezing attack that may otherwise disrupt it.

BODY LANGUAGE AND MANNERISMS

Perhaps too much has been made of the impact involuntary movements and gestures have on an interviewer and what they disclose about a candidate's motives and possible hidden agenda. Entire books are devoted to their variations and subtleties. Even so, what you do with your hands and face during the interview—albeit inadvertently—can sometimes be misinterpreted as an indication of possible absence of candor, or worse.

If you are trying to hide part of your past and think you can fool your interviewer—either by omission or commission—be advised that she has ways of countering your deception.

Dennis M. Kowal, a U.S. Army Intelligence psychologist, wrote in the human resources magazine *Personnel Journal* that 80 percent of communication is nonverbal rather than verbal, and that 80 percent of *that* communication shows itself in a person's face—particularly the eyes. He counsels interviewers to recognize the subtle nonverbal clues that indicate an attempt to deceive. Few applicants can lie without feeling a tightness in the stomach, which usually is manifested by an involuntary change in facial expression and a decrease of eye contact with the interviewer.

Sometimes nonverbal and verbal cues are combined. For example, a person will use an expression like "To tell the truth" or "To be perfectly honest," accompanied by a major break in eye contact, a shift in body orientation, or a movement of hand to face that results in an obvious physical contradiction.

Dishonesty has no place in the interview, obviously, and will probably be uncovered sooner or later anyway. The point is that because more and more interviewers are trained to recognize it, dishonesty becomes not only wrong but stupid.

Mannerisms

Many people aren't aware of facial tics or idiosyncratic mannerisms that may stand in the way of their making a positive first impression. If you have a doubt in this regard ask at least two friends or close family members to identify any possible physical distractions that may negatively affect your interviewing first impression. You may have a correctable physical, psychological, or neurological problem; but you won't be able to fix it until you have it diagnosed.

Other Causes of Fear and Discomfort

Most other reasons for feeling one would rather be anywhere but in an interview usually are grounded in a lack of preparation—either for the interview or for the job itself. This leads to a rapid drop in confidence, which in turn reveals itself in telltale body language.

After learning as much as you can about the job, the company, and the interviewer, examine your credentials. Be ready to defend your ability to handle any of your prospective responsibilities, including those you find out about for the first time in the interview.

Be able as well to identify and neutralize any possible weaknesses for the position you think you may have. Anticipating the worst that can happen and knowing how you will deal with it will lead to a peace of mind (or at least a reduction of panic) that will do wonders for your confidence level.

VOCABULARY AND DICTION

Some of you may argue that your job doesn't require sophisticated communication skills, which will sharply reduce any significance you might give to mastering the English language. The thing is, every job interviewee needs sufficient self-expression skills to get the job offer in the first place.

If a weakness in vocabulary or grammar is a problem of yours, remedy it at all costs. Minor gaps in your knowledge can be taken care of with assiduous study of a good, compact text, such as Strunk and White's *The Elements of Style*. (See also the recommended reading section at the end of this chapter, as well as numerous vocabulary improvement programs available in book and audio-tape format.) More serious problems will require formal study at a local community college or adult education center. Consult your telephone book Yellow Pages for a good institution nearby.

If you're unsure as to how serious your problem is, ask for permission to take a test at one of the two local sources mentioned above. On a day-to-day basis, carry a pocket dictionary with you or write down every word whose pronunciation or meaning you are unsure of, as a reminder to look them up at the end of the day.

Problems of New Citizens

Those of you for whom English is a second (or third) language face a more difficult problem. Not only will you have to demonstrate your facility for mastering a new tongue—with all of its implied nuances—but you must be perceived as acculturated enough to adapt quickly to your new supervisors, peers, and subordinates, as well. You may need to make a friend of someone in the industry you have selected, in order to familiarize yourself with professional colloquialisms, buzzwords, and vocabulary. This is tricky, of course, because such "In" words and phrases have a way of going out of fashion overnight. You'll be judged more harshly for using dated expressions and references than for staying with the tried, the true, and the generic.

Sometimes a candidate's accent or dialectic pattern calls attention to itself and distracts from the message. Minor problems can be corrected through numerous available audiotape programs. Individuals with accents so pronounced that understandability is a problem may need to consult a speech pathologist trained in accent reduction. For names of local specialists, check your Yellow Pages, hospital or clinic, or nearby university speech department.

PREPAREDNESS

One area of preparation that may affect a good first impression is embodied in a question that certainly will be asked early in the interview if your resume dates reveal an employment gap. (Resume strategies for this situation are dealt with in our companion book, *Conquer Resume Objections*.)

Here's the question: "I see on your resume that you left Animated Spirits in July. What was the situation there, by the way?"

If you have lost a job recently, you need to be able to answer this question—or any one of its many variations—in a way that satisfies your interviewer that your past will not adversely affect your future with her company.

This topic is thoroughly dealt with in Chapter 4, "Testing for Predictable Objections." We introduce it here because, if brought up early enough in your interview, it could mean a make-or-break first impression.

Write your own scenario in preparing to deal with your particular situation, making sure you cover each of the four points made on pages 61–63. Keep your script flexible, because you will be asked to explain your job loss in almost as many different ways as you will have interviews.

Never offer more information than you are asked; you risk appearing defensive by over-explaining. Answer direct questions honestly and with no unnecessary detail. Interviewers who want elaboration will ask for it. Finally, rehearse with your spouse or a friend various versions of your story, in various combinations of detail and with various emphases, until you are comfortable with it. (See Chapter 5 and Appendix B for case studies that may have crossover value for your situation.)

POOR LISTENING SKILLS

Far and away the most important interviewing skill to master is listening. It is especially important to listen carefully during the first minutes because your answers to the initial questions will set the tone for the rest of the meeting and determine the first impression you create.

The key to effective listening is concentration. Steel yourself to focus single-mindedly on the questions you are being asked, the way they are being asked, and any subtleties or hidden meanings that may lurk within them. Here are the most common examples of this attention lapse and how to prevent them.

Inattentiveness

Often a candidate's concentration will waver before the interviewer has finished the question, and in so doing, part of its meaning will be lost. Stay with the question until it is complete. Then frame your answer.

Missing Nuances

A friendly smile may mask a question behind the question, which you won't catch if your antennae are not up all the way. A frequently asked opening question like "Tell me about yourself," or one of its variations, sounds harmless enough. You'll lose points, though, if your response is rambling, halting, scattered, overlong or too detailed, is infused with personal rather than professional history, or repeats your resume entries. Your questioner wants to know what is important to you. Because the question is open-ended, you can answer it any way you want. Rehearse (but don't let it appear to sound so) a 15- or 20-second answer that is bare bones and hits the highlights of your professional career that best match the description of the *job you are there for*, as you know it. Skip childhood, college, marriage, and children; cut right to your growth record in the industry. (The interviewer probably has read your resume thoroughly, after all, and in all likelihood is looking at it while you speak.) "Tell me about yourself" is an opportunity for some creative packaging—and one of the few interview opportunities you will have for any control. (Look at Appendix A for four variations on the "Tell me about yourself" theme that you may want to adapt for your own purposes. They're written to accommodate the style of each of the four interviewer types described previously.)

Hearing What You Want to Hear

Not being completely prepared for your interview can cause your attention to wander while your interviewer asks her questions. This may happen if you want a job very badly and are overeager to make a good impression. If the reason for your overeagerness is that you are out of work and need a paycheck badly, you must sublimate your panic attack at all costs. Your state of mind will be obvious to your interviewer, and your chances of continuing as a viable candidate will be reduced to zero.

C. Hale Champion, former executive dean of Harvard's John F. Kennedy School of Government, says that sharing a frame of reference is the secret of an effective listener. The poor listener hears the other person's words only as a signal that it would be impolite to break in just yet. The good listener pays attention as he puts everything into an existing framework, gathering useful information but throwing out anything that doesn't fit. From then on, says Champion, he "isn't trying to put everything in his frame of reference but is instead trying to get his frame of reference adjusted to the person he is listening to."

ACTIVE LISTENING

Arthur Bell and Dayle Smith, in their book *Winning With Difficult People*,[1] talk about "active listening" as an alternative to anger when dealing with difficult people. Much of what they say is applicable to the hiring interview situation, beginning with first impressions to later stages of the interview. Bell and Smith describe two techniques to help put active listening into play. We've adapted them slightly for our purposes here:

Technique 1   At the outset, consciously turn off all prejudgments and assumptions about the interview. "Let it happen" in the same way a movie unfolds before you. Try to ask more questions than you usually do ("What do you mean?" "Tell me more about that." "Can you give me an example?")

Technique 2   Repeat some of the interviewer's key phrases to help clarify points you don't completely understand. Be sure your tone is one of interest, not judgment.

INTERVIEWER: A large part of the first several months, then, would be spent in fieldwork.

---

[1]Arthur H. Bell and Dayle M. Smith, *Winning With Difficult People* (Hauppauge, NY: Barron's Educational Series, Inc., 1991), pp. 35–36.

CANDIDATE: Fieldwork . . .

INTERVIEWER: Yes, fieldwork. Getting out into the territories to find out what the dealers are thinking . . . what their problems are. . . . This is what it will take to get this new product airborne.

Repeating words or phrases, in moderation, can be an effective alternative to the clarification questions asked in Technique 1. Still, the key word in the phrase "active listening" is "listening." Without your antennae out there, concentrating 100 percent for the duration of the interview, any additional tactics are rendered meaningless.

ADDITIONAL READING

Molloy, John T. *Dress for Success for Men*; and *The Women's Dress for Success Book*. New York: Warner Communications, 1978. The leading what-to-wear manual.

Snyder, Hal. *It Isn't Difficult to Be Outstanding: Personal Pocket Guide to Improving Sales Results*. New Providence, NJ: Quotable Communications, 1993. Thirty years of sales training experience distilled into 82 pages. See especially: "Key Contact Persons in the Sales Process" and "Customer Concerns," which parallel the most effective way to deal with an interviewer's objections.

3

Becoming the Ideal Candidate

Presenting yourself as the candidate best able to do the job presupposes a thorough knowledge of the job itself—or as many aspects of it as you can learn before and during the interview.

KNOW YOUR TARGET COMPANY'S PROBLEMS

This is sometimes a difficult concept to internalize. When a major pharmaceutical company needed to fill a top marketing position some time ago, it considered and screened dozens of candidates. After a two-month search, one individual seemed to stand out. In a similar position for a major competitor he had performed in exemplary fashion, with three promotions in eight years. From what the company could tell, he was a perfect fit. When the vice president of marketing asked the staffing manager to invite him in for an interview, the job was his to lose.

At 9:00 A.M. the following Tuesday, the employee designate appeared on schedule. After requisite small talk and coffee, the vice president of marketing asked him to describe his experience. Forty-five minutes later he had exhausted the topic with a virtual non-stop combination of entertaining war stories and descriptions of responsibilities. His body language and eye contact were excellent; his delivery, faultless—including an occasional pause for positive dramatic effect.

It was at this point that the marketing vice president had to excuse herself for another appointment, leaving the staffing manager to handle the official farewell. As she went out the door, the candidate turned to the staffing manager. "What do you think she's looking for?" he asked.

When the marketing vice president and the staffing manager met for lunch to debrief the morning interview, they agreed before the menus arrived that the candidate had struck out. Why?

To quote the vice president of marketing: "Why would I hire a person to identify my customer's needs when he wasn't smart enough to first find out what mine were?"

That is precisely the point. *If you don't find out what your prospective employer's problems are, there is no way for you to project yourself as the candidate best able to solve them.*

Easy for us to say when the interviewer holds all the cards, you're thinking? And when experts write books for *managers* describing the best ways to keep you in the dark about the nitty gritty of the opening, your job becomes even tougher. In his book *On Hiring,* for example, accounting recruiter Robert Half counsels interviewers "not to describe the job until *after* [emphasis his] you elicit information from the candidate. It's a tactical mistake in the early stages of the interview," he says, "to reveal details about the position, beyond a general job description."

Half's reasoning is that if details about the job are given away too soon, a candidate may be able to falsely tailor his background to the open job. If early in the conversation the interviewer says, for example, "We're looking for someone who is extremely well-organized and detail-minded," a shrewd candidate, according to Half, "will answer subsequent questions in a way calculated to give [the interviewer] the impression that he or she has those very qualities, whether they exist or not."

It seems unlikely that the shrewdest of candidates could get away with such empty bravado, even if questioned by a marginally competent interviewer. On the other hand, this is exactly the kind of information an interviewee must have to assure that he discusses those of his attributes that meet the employer's needs.

The point is that if you wait for the interviewer, you may not learn sufficient details about the position to present yourself as the ideal candidate. The interviewer has the power seat, after all, and too aggressive an effort on your part to change the course of the conversation may be interpreted negatively enough to knock you out of the running. A growing number of interviewers, moreover, are becoming schooled in this cat-and-mouse game, which will surely do little to make your job easier.

So let's cut right to the ways you can most effectively communicate all of your job-related strengths in a way that projects you as the ideal candidate—then test to make sure you have done so. There are six good ways to stay on top of the interview and give yourself the best opportunity to become the ideal candidate.

1. Answer the interviewer's questions succinctly, leaving time for your own follow-up questions.
2. Prepare your questions beforehand.
3. Ask questions that fully define the job.
4. Take notes to be sure you retain crucial information.
5. Listen for the questions **behind** the questions.
6. Summarize periodically to test for thoroughness and accuracy.

Prepare Your Questions Beforehand

Be sure you know what you want to get out of the interview before you go in. All of the unknown factors related to job, company, and prospective boss that have not emerged through your research should become part of your list. Go back to Chapter 1 to review the kinds and levels of information that will be helpful to you.

Classify your questions by category and write them on 3 x 5 cards. Here are a few categories that might call for separate cards:

Job

- Unrevealed Responsibilities
- Potential for Growth
- Quality of "Team" (superiors, subordinates, peers)
- Biggest Immediate Challenges
- Biggest Long-term Challenges

Company

- Short-term Prospects
- Long-term Prospects
- Problems

Boss

- Time on the Job
- Track Record
- Management Style
- Strengths and Weaknesses

Hiring agenda

- Number of active candidates
- Number to be selected for second interview
- Timetable for next interview

Stay away from salary and benefits questions until all questions about the job itself have been resolved. Any premature interest in the compensation package will be interpreted as giving a higher priority to the paycheck than to professional growth.

Ask Questions That Define the Job

Step two is to find places in the interview that allow you to ask questions of your own. Extremely structured interviewers who ask only the questions on the list in front of them—and don't stray from the sequence—will be more difficult to work with than those who are less formal. But in either case, start with general, open-ended questions and work your way into the specifics.

Here first is a failed attempt to illuminate the job with good questions. Before looking at the end of the chapter for the reasons for failure, see if you can come up with them on your own.

The premise: an architect is interviewing for an assignment to design an office in the home of a self-employed consultant.

INTERVIEWER: Well, here's the space. As you can see, it has a lot of potential. I have some ideas, but mostly I'd like to hear yours.

ARCHITECT: You're right. This could become the most interesting room in the house. (Opens portfolio.) Here, let me show you what I've done for other clients in town. Here's a kitchen I designed 10 years ago. A living room a few years ago over on Prospect Street. Here's an interesting family room I designed. This deck gave me fits—see that rock I had to work around?

INTERVIEWER: I know we have to figure just how much additional weight the existing frame can carry. Is that going to be a real problem?

ARCHITECT: Not to worry. I'll do the whole thing.

INTERVIEWER: You'll draw up a set of plans, too?

ARCHITECT: No problem.

So why didn't the architect get the job? To find out, turn to page 55.

Hint: The relationship we want to encourage between interviewee and interviewer is closer to that of a professional seeking an assignment from a client than a prospective employee asking for a job from an employer.

Now here is a more successful approach, assuming you've done your homework:

INTERVIEWER: Have you been waiting long? I got held up down the hall.

CANDIDATE: Oh, about 20 minutes, I guess. Actually, it gave me a little extra time to reread my notes about Ajax's exit from the valve cover market. By the way, how might that affect the purchasing position you're looking to fill?

or,

INTERVIEWER: Sorry I had to change the appointment time. This has been a very different kind of week.

CANDIDATE: Actually, those extra days gave me time to learn more about Buckfinder's new involvement in asset-based financing. Am I right in assuming that this is one of the areas you'll want your new marketing manager to get into?

INTERVIEWER: Yes, indeed. Have you been exposed to asset-based financing to any degree?

CANDIDATE: I have, yes. Three products I managed were aimed at prospective clients with a large volume of receivables to invest.

INTERVIEWER: Oh, this is good to know. But back to your resume for a moment . . .

Be on the lookout for any wedge that will permit you to get in a point or two of your own. Without trying to "take control" of the interview—or even give the slightest perception of *attempting* control—it is possible to get your position-defining questions into the conversation. Rather then interrupting the interviewer's rhythm by asking a question out of context, though, follow one of your answers with a *related* question that will give you more insight to the job.

Early questions may cover your first job after school, rather than your current position. Many interviewers like to start at the beginning of a candidate's career and work forward, the opposite of the way most resumes are put together. This gives them a more cohesive look at the candidate's professional progress, as well as a way to see how it was measured. In any case, here are a few ways for you to turn the edge.

INTERVIEWER: I see that you put together a whole new accounts receivable system while you were at Baby Bell. Tell me a little bit about how that came about.

CANDIDATE: Well, at that time I was the only one in the department with any computer background to speak of. When I saw how slowly reports were getting out, I suggested to my boss that we put in a computerized system using Lotus. She gave me the go-ahead, and two months later we were in business. Is there a similar problem to be solved here at Comtel, or were you more interested in the way I handled innovation at Baby Bell?

[The candidate has asked the interviewer to clarify the purpose of the question. Her answer will give him another key piece of information to help define the position.]

INTERVIEWER: I see that you changed territories three times in five years when you were with Carstairs. Did any of these transfers involve training new people?

CANDIDATE: One of the switches had to do with a realignment of territories and actually involved combining two territories in one. The other two were promotions to larger operations. There was no need to train anyone in either case.

So the short answer is "no, I didn't do any training at Carstairs." I am a good trainer, though, and have had some good solid experience. Would training be a significant part of the job here?

INTERVIEWER: You bet. I need someone to bring a few younger people along.

CANDIDATE: In that case, let me tell you about the sales-people I worked with at Nuntendo . . .

[It's possible that the interviewer would have been more direct in her inquiry about the importance of the training function in the new job. But maybe not. You can't afford to take the chance and risk that the interviewer not know how good you are—for every key aspect of the position. If you did not know previously about a relatively obscure component of the job that your resume does not stress, you risk losing the opportunity without knowing why.]

INTERVIEWER: And that's about it. Do you have any other questions?

CANDIDATE: A few, yes. What's going to be the toughest part of this job, do you think?

INTERVIEWER: I think getting a handle on any campaign as quickly as possible. Sitting with our line people in each of the businesses and translating their needs and problems into products that communicate and solve these problems.

CANDIDATE: That's encouraging. In fact, that was all a good part of my job description at Frycook Central. By the way, here are a few pieces from the FastFry product line I mentioned earlier that may be relevant here. Would you like to see the telemarketing proposal I put together? That campaign has been out for more than six months, so there's nothing proprietary about it.

[Learning the most demanding aspects of the job allows a candidate to present himself in terms of actual challenges and thus improve his chances of getting a job offer.]

INTERVIEWER: Anything else?

CANDIDATE: One other thing. I also wanted to ask: Can you visualize the ideal candidate? I mean, what are the top three or four qualities you're looking for?

INTERVIEWER: Let's see. An exposure to investment banking, which you have—at least marginally. Good communications skills; an ability to work well with a variety of personalities and special backgrounds. Good analytical skills, and an ability to inspire and motivate.

CANDIDATE: I think I can demonstrate all of those characteristics, and there are people who will testify to those that I haven't convinced you of here. Is there one you'd like me to discuss at this time?

INTERVIEWER: Yes, as a matter of fact. We've talked some about investment banking. Maybe you could walk me through each of the others.

[Sometimes it isn't necessary to probe to find out how closely you match the description of the ideal candidate. Simply ask the question and you get the information. In the illustration above, the most effective response would be to tick off an example in your background that matches each of the top qualities the interviewer has mentioned. The next most effective is to be sure you have internalized all of the characteristics mentioned and document your ability to perform the tasks they represent—then reinforce them at the end of the interview, or in writing or by telephone subsequent to the interview.]

Take Notes to Retain Crucial Information

You may have heard that taking notes in a job interview is a bad idea: that you'll be judged as too dense to retain information without cribbing; that you'll lose focus on key points the interviewer is making; that you'll distract the interviewer through the physical act of writing, and thereby be labeled inconsiderate or unprofessional.

Almost none of this is true. Except for the occasional unin-
formed or inexperienced interviewer, rarely will you be faulted for
keeping track of important information. It isn't as though the interviewer will be providing you with a transcript of interview highlights, after all. You are completely on your own.

If you have the slightest doubt about your ability to keep everything in your head, bring out the pad and pencil the first time
things seem to be moving too fast for you. As you do so, pause and
ask: "Do you mind if I take notes?" You can be relatively sure the
answer will be "no." Ask your interviewer to repeat anything you
don't fully absorb. Neither your attention span nor your retentive
powers will be called into question. Concentrate on recording key
words that you can flesh out in more comprehensive fashion after
the interview. For example, the key words in the interviewer's
description of the job on page 48 are:

"investment banking"

"communication skills"

"work with variety of people"

"analytical skills"

"ability to inspire and motivate"

Use any shorthand that you'll be able to decipher after the
interview.

Listen for the Questions *Behind* the Questions

Listening is as important at this stage of the interview as it was back
when you were trying to make the best first impression. At this
stage, however, you'll be almost totally occupied with nuances. A
good part of your task must include knowing *why* a particular
question was asked before you decide how to answer—somewhat
more challenging than absorbing straightforward descriptions of
your prospective duties.

Your candidacy probably will be tested indirectly as well as
directly. Such qualities as motivation, insight, planning abilities,
and initiative may be analyzed through questions that appear to be
less probing than that. Management Recruiters, a nationwide executive recruitment firm, has prepared a guide to assist its clients

with questions that put the light on candidates in terms of assessing those qualities listed above. Here are a few examples from each of these categories—slightly modified for our purposes:

(What They Ask) **(What They're Looking For)**

MOTIVATION

How will this job help you get what you want?

What are your priorities?

What have you done to prepare yourself for a better job?

How motivated are you?

INITIATIVE

How did you get into this line of work?

Are you a self-starter?

When was the last time you felt like giving up on a task? Tell me about it.

Can you complete an unpleasant assignment?

INSIGHT

What is the most useful criticism you've received? Tell me about it. The least useful?

Can you take and utilize criticism?

How do you handle fault-finders?

How do you handle criticism?

PLANNING

Give me an idea of how you spend a typical day.

Will you fit readily into our corporate culture and organizational structure?

If you were boss, how would you run your department? How did you get into this line of work?

Do you have vision, or will you get bogged down by detail?

Summarize Periodically

To effectively pick up all key points your interviewer makes, summarize each major topic, and use test connectors to be sure you're right. For example:

"Let me see if I've got this straight . . . "

"Do you mind if I try to paraphrase that last point . . . ?"

or,

"O.K. Is this an accurate summary of what you just said . . . ?"

Questions like these will be helpful in putting a semicolon to your conversation, so that you can accurately digest what has gone before. Notes you've already taken should be helpful at this point, as well. If your interviewer agrees with your summary, just move into any response you may have without shifting gears. If she makes a correction or adds a thought, listen carefully, probe and clarify if necessary, then respond. This way you not only fine tune your understanding, but communicate the importance you attach to what the interviewer is saying.

Before we leave the subject of listening, don't minimize the positive effect an ability to relax can have on your performance. Being well prepared is the single ingredient leading to ready relaxation. But this you already know if you remember the advice offered in Chapter 1.

With this freedom from the worry of "Will I screw up the next question?" or "Can I do this job?" you'll be able to spend more time on the nuances of a question, or ask an intelligent question of your own about an area of the job or company that you know less about than you want to.

A NEW GENERATION OF INTERVIEWERS

Because our nation's soft economy over the past decade has led to an unprecedented number of unemployed workers—and therefore to an ever-growing talent pool of available men and women— companies are becoming more and more rigorous in codifying the employee selection process. For this reason the job-search challenge is becoming increasingly complex for everyone looking for a new or better job.

Connecticut's Pratt & Whitney, a division of United Technologies, is one of a number of companies to have devised an extremely comprehensive matrix for assessing potential new managers—as well as candidates who indicate managerial possibilities. Individuals are rated in six evaluation categories, with a number of subcategories to consider for each:

Achievement

- Attains objectives on schedule
- Meets or exceeds achievement objectives
- Follows through and persists despite obstacles

Managing Change

- Develops and implements decisions leading to change
- Executes decisions in logical, timely fashion
- Takes calculated risks

Leading by Example

- Adheres to business and personal principles
- Meets or exceeds high performance standards
- Exhibits leadership across functional boundaries

Creating a Shared Vision

- Perceives and integrates business issues
- Communicates vision to organization

Building Constructive Relationships

- Displays sound judgment in staff selection, assignment, and delegation
- Shows respect for others
- Demonstrates sound communication skills

Technical Competence

- Acquires, processes and applies knowledge to applicable business opportunities and problems

For each open position at Pratt & Whitney, a hiring team reviews the candidates identified for the position and selects those it wants to interview. The team leader (usually the hiring executive) is responsible for seeing that the rest of the team is familiar with the process.

All first-time interviewers attend a one-on-one planning session with a lead interviewer and sit in on a number of live interviews before conducting one of their own. The group decides which aspects of the interview will be handled by each member.

Let's say each team member is responsible for one of the key evaluation categories mentioned above. The individual handling, say, "Managing Change" will have a list of questions and suggested additional observation tools and thus be able to report in depth on that aspect of each candidate's merit. For example:

Interview Questions

- Provide examples of key business decisions you have made in your career.
- What were the factors leading to the decision? The causes and effects? The information available? The timing? What was learned?
- Give examples of innovative approaches you have used to accomplish work tasks.
- What are some of the most striking examples of business risk-taking you have engaged in?
- What were the key factors in the situation, the process used to assess risk, the specific actions taken, the outcomes, and the lessons learned from the experience?

Other Observation Methods

- Solicit business plans from the candidate and review them for evidence of judgment and planned results.

- Review candidate's resume for examples of technical, organizational, or personal innovation.

- Ask the candidate's manager for examples of risk-taking (either explicit or implicit) by candidate in business plans, descriptions of business results, or work.

Today's job market is loaded in favor of the buyer and may be so for several years. To get a job with a company that realizes this, you may be put to rigorous tests as pressures mount to hire only the best. The equivocal, superficial answers often suggested for "tough interviewer questions" will be of little use with some of today's more sophisticated interviewers. To become the ideal candidate in such situations, you'll need to be able to seamlessly integrate all of the subtleties and transferable qualities of your professional background with the requirements of the job at hand.

CJA Career Services, in its publication *Staffing: The Bottom Line*, lists six "core traits" managers should look for in a candidate:

1. Deep-rooted personal values
2. A strong sense of responsibility
3. A high level of self-esteem
4. A probing approach to problem-solving
5. Persuasiveness
6. Strong interpersonal skills[1]

Projecting these characteristics and skill sets will go a good distance toward offsetting minor flaws that may surface in your candidacy.

QUALIFYING THE JOB, THE COMPANY, AND THE BOSS

The flip side of becoming the ideal candidate is to determine whether you are interviewing for the ideal job. Go back to Chapter 1 of *Conquer Resume Objections* to review the criteria for deciding whether to pursue a job. At this point you'll probably have just a ballpark

---

[1]Cunningham, Jacob, Adler & Associates, Inc., Tustin, CA.

knowledge of the compensation package (if more than base salary is involved), but all other qualifiers should be thoroughly analyzed.

ANSWER TO QUESTION ON PAGE 45

(What did the architect do that caused him to lose the office design job?)

- He was so focused on his past accomplishments that he failed to deal with the assignment at hand. He needed to find out first how the client wanted the space used. "Have you thought about using skylights?" "Have you considered using dormers, or lifting the roof?" "Do you want one large room or separated spaces?" "What is your budget?" "What is your timetable?" "Have you already assigned a builder (contractor)?"
- With answers to questions like these, the next steps would have become clear. Even so, the architect could have said: "Let me think about this for a while. I'd like to take some measurements and come back next week with two or three possible solutions. That would be the best time for me to hear some of your ideas so that we could integrate them."
- The architect needed to find out what the client's needs and requirements were, and then describe himself in terms of these requirements.

ADDITIONAL READING

Anthony, Medley H. *Sweaty Palms: The Neglected Art of Being Interviewed.* Berkeley, CA: Ten Speed Press, 1992. How a properly prepared candidate's strengths can make a lasting first impression; tips for projecting honesty, confidence, and employability; handling sexual harassment and discrimination.

Beatty, Richard H. *The Five Minute Interview: A New and Powerful Approach to Interviewing.* New York: John Wiley & Sons, Inc., 1986. A variation of the approach recommended in Chapter 3:

discover the employer's real needs and objections, and position yourself accordingly.

Wilson, Robert F. *Conducting Better Job Interviews*. Hauppauge, NY: Barron's Educational Series, Inc., 1991. Secrets from the other side of the desk. What new managers are taught about how to choose the best person for the job.

4

Testing for Predictable Objections

The odds are that at some point—maybe not in the first interview; it could even be the second or third—the interviewer will decide that you are not the best person for the job. The more candidates there are for the open position, obviously, the greater this probability is.

Ironically, this could happen even though you have followed every bit of advice in this book so far, and *are* the best person for the job.

Dealing head-on with an objection to your candidacy is a process largely missing in most books on job-search strategy, or counsel from executive recruiters and outplacement firms. Yet it is a central element in any worthwhile sales training program, and we think it will be useful to you here. Overcoming objections is completely consistent, after all, with our view that a job interview closely resembles a business meeting between a buyer and a seller. In any effectively run sales meeting the seller must work to overcome all of the buyer's objections to purchasing the product or service.

Recently the authors led two one-day seminars on job interviewing for alumni of an Ivy League graduate school of business. All of the seventy-plus attendees were in one stage or another of career transition. Some had recently lost jobs; others had decided to make a professional change and wanted to improve or refreshen their job-search tools.

The professional experience level of group members ranged from five months to twenty-five years. Among them were lawyers, investment bankers, marketing managers, and executives from both manufacturing- and service-oriented organizations. At the time, some of those who were out of work were being assisted by the most prestigious outplacement firms in the industry—or recently had undergone that experience.

Yet, according to the results of a survey taken at the end of the day for each of the two groups, the idea of identifying and neutralizing interviewer objections had occurred to none of these people before they arrived at the seminar. Indeed, most were extremely uncomfortable with the concept and many of them strongly resisted our efforts to help them deal with it. After they had gone through the process, though, the attendees on both days rated "Overcoming Objections" one of the most effective and powerful interviewing tools they had learned. In a follow-up survey six months later, several of the workshop members attributed job offers they had received to the mastery of overcoming objections.

RECRUITERS KNOW OBJECTIONS

Candidates for open positions working with effective executive recruiters have less to worry about than those relying solely on their own marketing skills.

Corporate clients judge recruiters by the quality of the candidates they present. For this reason, good recruiters realize it is in their best interest to find out as much about their candidates as possible, both to minimize surprises in the interview and to better match candidates against the employer's requirements—first prize, of course, going to The Ideal Candidate. Therefore, they need a warts-and-all, three-dimensional portrait of anyone they think has a real shot at the job. This allows them to field all objections, neutralizing all they can. This is how they earn their fees.

If you get the opportunity, ask your recruiter how he does it. Tips from the pros can help a lot. Many job seekers, however, won't have the opportunity to work with a recruiter. If this is you, pay particular attention to the rest of this chapter and to all of Chapter 5.

TYPES OF INTERVIEWER OBJECTIONS

The kinds of objections you will face in any interview can be narrowed down to four. Rather than describe them here with a full range of examples, however, we'll touch briefly on each type and follow with a section describing the complete process for resolving objections. Case studies of objections provided *after* you learn the process will make it easier for you to apply them to your situation.

Chapter 4 covers basic objections and suggestions for dealing with them. Chapter 5 takes a more complex level of objection. Frequently, the interviewer will not be willing to share her *real* concern with you, which makes the objection considerably more difficult to deal with. We'll attempt to help you identify the interviewer's real concerns and suggest strategies for bringing your candidacy back to life. The four kinds of objections are those that the interviewer:

1. Thought of and asked
2. Thought of and didn't ask
3. Thought of but couldn't legally ask
4. Thought of after the interview

Objections Thought of and Asked

This is the easiest type of objection to deal with. One common example is a statement at variance with a resume entry. It can often result from a simple misunderstanding or misstatement and is easily put right. Simply apologize, restate the fact (along with any obvious reason for your error), and move on. For example:

CANDIDATE: So I created a 320-store test to analyze customer buying patterns, and this allowed us to maximize our inventory investment quite effectively.

INTERVIEWER: (Pause.) But according to your resume this was a *120*-store test. Is there something I'm missing?

CANDIDATE: Oh, I'm sorry. The test itself took place in 120 stores. When that worked out as well as it did, we implemented the program in all 320 stores over the next six months. Sorry I wasn't clear about that.

INTERVIEWER: Oh, I see. No problem.

Overcoming a Job Loss Objection

If you've lost your job recently, you can be sure the interviewer will ask you about it. Job loss was first mentioned in Chapter 3 to illustrate how thorough preparation for discussing an unpleasant topic can generate a comfort level in the interview that can in turn lead to a good first impression. Let's go through a scenario that may suggest tactics to help you overcome this objection when the time comes:

INTERVIEWER: I see that you left Universal Joints in July. How did that come about?

CANDIDATE: Actually, I was dismissed.

INTERVIEWER: Oh? What was the situation there?

CANDIDATE: Well, it seemed that my boss and I had very different workways. He replaced the previous group manager who had hired me.

INTERVIEWER: What do you mean, the two of you had "very different workways?"

CANDIDATE: Well, he wanted a lot more frequent feedback than I was used to providing. With my previous boss I was in the habit of just doing the best job I could on my own after I was clear about the department's objectives. My new boss had other expectations. He wanted to be briefed on a daily basis. This was a constant tension between us.

INTERVIEWER: What happened, specifically?

CANDIDATE: I had seen a few of the danger signs a couple of months earlier, but obviously I didn't do enough about them to change the situation. Actually, things had been getting worse for about six months, and then bingo—I was gone.

INTERVIEWER: How do you view the experience with the hindsight you have now?

CANDIDATE: It was a fundamental learning experience, I can tell you that. Maybe I was a little bit arrogant. I don't know. I certainly was shortsighted. Underneath it all, I probably was taking out my resentment on my new boss. I really liked the guy who had hired me, and I thought he had been treated unfairly. Bottom line is, I know what went wrong and I know it won't happen again. The experience has taught me to be a much better communicator. Would you like any more detail than this?

INTERVIEWER: No, thank you. I appreciate your frank response.

The candidate followed four basic principles in neutralizing a job loss objection, as identified in the career transition program *Job-Bridge*:[1]

1. *Don't knock your former employer.* Many victims of job loss blame former employers for their troubles. This is especially true of very recent terminees, who often spend so much time grieving about their last job that they render themselves impotent in their search for a new one. Following this route invariably stamps you, accurately or not, as a vindictive whiner unable to put the past behind you.

2. *Don't dwell on negatives.* Appearing to wallow in the misfortune of your most recent job experience similarly conveys the message that your past supersedes the present in terms of your priorities. No meaningful search for employment can move forward until you expel the residue from a bad last job.

3. *Accept responsibility you deserve.* Look within yourself for the maturity and introspection to examine your last employment situation objectively. List and acknowledge the pivotal mistakes you made and how much they may have contributed to the loss of your job. This level of detachment may require some help from one or more of your former colleagues. Ask for brutal honesty, to be sure

---

[1]*Job-Bridge*, New Haven, CT: Wilson McLeran, Inc., This is a multimedia program.

you are not protecting yourself from any responsibility you rightfully deserve. Then be certain you can handle the honesty, in case it contradicts your still subjective recollections.

4. *Identify positive outcomes.* Marshaling your total efforts for a job search can be effective only after you reach closure from your previous job. Analyze the reasons for your mistakes and establish a game plan for translating them into learning experiences you can take to your next job and profit from.

Your story may bear no resemblance to the hypothetical example scripted on pages 60 and 61, but the four principles should be adhered to without exception.

Don't rely on a memorized, word-for-word presentation to get through this interview land mine. First of all, unless you are a superb actor your response will *sound* memorized—and by definition will be suspect. Instead, prepare answers—in substance, not word for word—to as many questions as you can think of related to the reason(s) you lost your job.

Your answers will vary, of course, with your situation. Not only that—different interviewers will ask for differing amounts of detail, depending on their perspective. For this reason your answers should be structured on a "need to know" basis: most relevant information first, with less important details following, and only if the interviewer asks for them. Structure all of your answers with the four principles of overcoming a job loss objection just discussed firmly in mind. Here are a few ways this objection might be phrased:

- Why do you think things got as bad as they did?
- What do you think you could have done to change things that you didn't do?
- To what extent was your job performance an issue, do you think?
- Why weren't you able to get along with your boss? (or with whomever else there may have been a problem)
- Couldn't you see this coming?
- Why did it take you so long to get a handle on the situation?
- When you saw that your job was in jeopardy, why didn't you go to your boss about it? (If your relationship with your

boss *was* the problem: "Would it have been politically possible for you to go to your boss's boss?"; or "Wasn't there a colleague you could have asked to intercede on your behalf?")

- Have you had similar problems in other jobs?
- Now that you have this experience behind you, what would you have done differently, do you think?

The key is to be so well prepared that you can answer all questions calmly and assertively—meanwhile keeping in mind the four principles of neutralizing a job loss objection.

Objections Thought of But Not Asked

Sometimes you'll have to dig to learn about aspects of your candidacy that may concern the interviewer. Most of us have a tendency to withhold bad news. It is unpleasant and tends to embarrass us.

Put yourself in the interviewer's shoes. Think how much more difficult it must be to verify a flaw we think we see in a candidate's character, personality, or level of competency by confronting him about it. More frequently an interviewer will make a judgment about the candidate and look for verbal and nonverbal clues to support and reinforce that judgment, but not bring up the objection directly. This means that the interviewer's case is built solely on inference, with the candidate denied an opportunity to refute the unspoken charges.

Look back at the example in the previous section. The interviewer noticed a discrepancy between the candidate's resume entry and his recollection of the number of stores he tested to analyze customer buying patterns. If the interviewer had said nothing, but simply stored this apparent discrepancy for later reference, the candidate would not have had an opportunity to refute it. The interviewer would retain an erroneous judgment of the candidate's integrity, which probably would kill any chance for a job offer. Chapter 5 is devoted entirely to objections that were not asked for one reason or another—such as the one introduced in the last paragraph of the next section.

Objections Thought of That Couldn't Legally Be Asked

The third kind of objection relates to questions the interviewer may want to ask but would be liable for a discrimination charge if she did so. It is unlawful, for example, to:

- Refuse to consider for employment any person because of race, color, national origin, religion, sex, age, handicap, covered veteran status, or physical disability.

- Categorize job candidates on the basis of race, color, national origin, sex, religion, or age.

- Exhibit bias in employment advertising based on race, color, national origin, sex, religion, or age.

- Use any screening techniques (questionnaires and tests, for example), that are not directly job-related.

The consequences of violating Equal Employment Opportunity Commission ordinances are severe. One large law firm was recently barred from recruiting at the University of Chicago for a year following a black law student's complaint that racist questions had been asked of her while she was interviewing for a position with the firm. Individuals who believe they have been discriminated against during any recruitment process have 300 days to file a complaint.

Obviously the human resource professionals you interview with will be better informed regarding EEOC regulations than will most line managers. When your principles dictate, then, you have every right to point out violations or to take action following the interview.

The dilemma results, of course, when there is information the interviewer refrains from asking that you are not reluctant to provide. Suppose you are interviewing for a job and are a single parent with three children at home. You may sense that the interviewer would like to know how you would handle a possible child-care problem but cannot legally request this information. You might voluntarily explain how you are handling this challenge and eliminate one obstacle to getting the job. (See Chapter 5 for an example.)

Objections Thought of After the Interview

Everybody experiences second thoughts, even interviewers. The difficulty lies in trying to anticipate them. By asking the interviewer questions such as the following, it will be possible to avoid those objections that may have occurred to the interviewer just before she fell asleep the night of your interview:

"Is there anything else we should discuss?"

or,

"Do you have any further questions?"

or,

"Is there anything I've left out?"

Beyond this you've gone as far as you can; there isn't a great deal more you can do except to find out when the next round of interviews will be scheduled. Specific suggestions on this and other topics related to the end of the job-search process will be found in Chapter 6.

Using Questions to Neutralize Objections

Objections of any kind can be overcome by providing the appropriate information at the appropriate time. Let's say you have identified three specific job requirements the successful candidate must fill. Your task is to select from your background only those accomplishments and skills that match the requirements and demonstrate your competence in them as effectively as you can. Everything else is extraneous and has no place in your presentation.

After dealing with each of the requirements, try to reach closure and make sure your presentation was successful. The interviewer may interrupt you with additional questions to help her clarify points you were in the process of making, before you complete your answer.

"How many people were you supervising at this point?"

or,

"What was your production goal?"

or,

"To what extent were you able to reduce your scrap rate?"

There are questions designed to clarify, not to put you on the spot. The trick is not to "lose your place" when you are interrupted, and be able to come back to the point of departure.

Smoking Out Objections

But whether you're asked such clarifying questions or not, ask your own closure question at the end of each topic covered to be sure there are no residual objections. For example:

"Is there anything else I can add?"

or,

"Does that cover the topic, as far as you're concerned?"

or,

"What more would you like to know?"

or,

"Have I left anything out, from your point of view?"

After you have completed your presentation of all of the requirements as you understand them, ask a similar question to see if you can identify cumulative doubts about your ability to handle the job. For example: "I believe I've covered the three requirements you outlined. Is there more I can add about any one of them—or is there anything else we should cover?"

OVERCOMING OBJECTIONS—THE PROCESS

Now that you have a better idea of the reasons for your interviewer's objections, you need to be able to analyze them to take appropriate action. Here is the resolution sequence that will apply to most objections:

- Understand the objection

- Acknowledge the objection
- Neutralize the objection

All steps won't be necessary in every case. Use them all only when you need to.

Listen to Understand the Objection

Your most valuable interviewing skill, listening, is particularly applicable here. Having all of your antennae out will allow you to gather more data. This will indicate to the interviewer that you value her concern or hesitancy. By listening carefully, you communicate respect. This, in turn, will encourage the interviewer to ask questions that get at areas of your candidacy that may be troublesome to her.

By listening patiently, rather than responding with the first thought that pops into your head, you may discover that the initial question masked the real objection. If you don't understand the question, say so. For example:

"Could you expand on that? A few more details would help me understand your concern."

Listening carefully to the restatement of her concern tells the interviewer that you think what she wants to find out is more important than what you came prepared to say. You have made her agenda *your* agenda, which in some cases may have been the root of her original concern.

Acknowledge the Objection

Acknowledge the objection by restating it in your own words. This step gives you a chance to either dispel the interviewer's objection on the spot, or paraphrase it to be sure you completely understand the general concern being raised:

"In other words, you don't think I was on that job long enough to pick up the vendor contact experience you're looking for. Is that my biggest problem, do you think?"

or,

"I see. You're doubtful that I can rely on just my on-the-job background without an M.B.A. to back it up. Is that your major concern?"

An affirmative response tells you what the problem is. Now you are able to explore the issues that underlie the stated objection. You can gather additional information as well as communicate to your interviewer that you want to fully understand the depth of her concern. As we have seen, sometimes the interviewer is reluctant to state the real objection. She may be leaning toward another candidate, but out of fairness feel an obligation to complete your interview anyway. This gives you an uphill battle, but also tells you what you have to do to win it.

Most interviewees believe that bringing up negative aspects of their candidacy can do nothing but scuttle their chances for a job offer. Partly this is fear of dealing with a topic they believe can only hurt them; partly it is wishful thinking. (If we don't talk about my shortcomings, maybe they won't become a factor.) Such thinking ignores the fact that until all of an interviewer's negative feelings are *verbalized* and subsequently *resolved*, they fester, magnify, and become a dominant reason for rejection.

When you fish for objections, it is important not to play prosecuting attorney but to ask your questions in a calm, patient manner. Your objective is to get to the source of the interviewer's concerns—but not to the extent that you weaken your fragile relationship with her.

Sometimes you both need more information. She needs to learn more about you, and you need to know more about the nature of her unresolved doubt. This exchange may not eradicate all concern, but it will prepare you both for the next step.

Neutralize the Objection

Now that the interviewer knows you have taken the time to hear her out and acknowledge her concern, she is ready for any information that will resolve it. Answer fully, with no hint of defensiveness.

Let's say you're trying to make a move from one industry or discipline to another at the same level. Your interviewer's objections usually are all legitimate, and exist because she is trying to visualize your skills and background being successfully applied to an unfamiliar work environment.

Your final task is to determine whether you have effectively overcome the objection. The only way to do this is to ask, and then count on your powers of observation to decide whether you're getting a complete, honest answer:

"Does that answer cover all of the ground you wanted it to?"

or,

"Is there anything you'd like me to add to that?"

or,

"What more can I tell you?"

The response you receive to summary questions such as these will give you immediate feedback as to whether you've satisfactorily overcome the objection.

If the response to your summary question is ambiguous or equivocal in any way, though, you may have to continue your effort beyond the interview. This could consist of "evidence" you volunteer at the end of the interview that sufficiently neutralizes the objection; or it could take the form of a letter that outlines your response in measured, documented fashion.

Here's an example that incorporates applicable objection resolution steps, and is precipitated by the candidate asking a probing question. The interviewer is about to end the meeting when the candidate thinks to ask if there are any objections to his candidacy:

INTERVIEWER: Well, if there are no more questions . . .

CANDIDATE: No, I think we've covered everything I wanted to know about. Is there anything I've said that gave you less than total confidence in my ability to do the job?

INTERVIEWER: I don't believe so. You're probably not as strong in the area of long-range planning as I would like, but I don't see that as being a critical factor.

CANDIDATE: Oh, really? I guess that's an area we didn't discuss in great detail, and it obviously bears on this job. A couple of months before I was given that special project at Rogueworks

I told you about, I was asked to come up with a rationale that would either justify the project or cause us to scrap it. The team I put together crafted the plan they finally went with. I could show it to you—it's no longer proprietary. Would you like to hear more?

INTERVIEWER: If your plan is as good as you say it is, that should do it. By the way, I'm glad you asked.

CANDIDATE: So am I.

The candidate was able to resolve the interviewer's lingering doubts about his experience in the area of long-range planning because he:

1. Asked specifically if there were any objections to his candidacy
2. Listened carefully to the interviewer's response
3. Acknowledged his understanding of the objection
4. Cited a specific job experience and accomplishment he believed would neutralize the objection
5. Re-asked his question to ensure that his previous response had solved the problem

In Chapter 5 we will learn more about how to neutralize the complex objections, mostly those the interviewer thought of, but did not—or felt she could not—ask. Meantime, here are a few objections candidates frequently face in their first interviews.

OBJECTION-ILLUMINATING QUESTIONS

Interviewers use calculated lines of questioning to illuminate candidate weaknesses, thereby either highlighting or eliminating a number of areas of concern. The following scenarios illustrate ways these scenes can be played out. Some are based on actual candidate-interviewer discussions (or in one case, a post-interview letter); others are hypothetical. All are based on perceived objections that need to be neutralized.

Objection: Lack of persistence

INTERVIEWER: You thought you "weren't going to make it?" What do you mean?

CANDIDATE: Well, when I graduated from college I started as a door-to-door salesman, and at first was rejected 40 times for every time I heard the word "yes." Before the year was out I was able to get the ratio down to 20-to-one.

INTERVIEWER: How did that compare to the average for your group?

CANDIDATE: At first, I was toward the bottom, but I finally got good enough so I was getting awards for my sales rate.

INTERVIEWER: Why do you think you succeeded?

CANDIDATE: At first it was purely out of fear. I did not want to fail, because that would mean that I'd get fired.

In our first day of training, the instructor said: "Look at the person on your right . . . now on your left. Look at the person behind you . . . now the person in front of you. At the end of this year, only one of the five of you will be left." He was right—and I was one of the few who made it.

INTERVIEWER: When did the "fear," as you call it, wear off? What replaced it?

CANDIDATE: When I said "fear," I didn't mean fear of rejection—that comes with the territory, so to speak. I was afraid of failing. What I finally realized was, after I mastered the techniques it was simply a game of numbers. Then I just buckled down and did the job. The more doors I knocked on, the better my odds. I tried different techniques for each situation, and after a while I learned which techniques improved the odds in which situations.

INTERVIEWER: Is that the key to your success: seeing as many potential customers as you can, and a mastery of the selling techniques?

CANDIDATE: Initially it was, yes. But as I grew more experienced, a third factor came into play: knowledge of industry and product.

Critique: From the interviewer's questions, the candidate realized that his ability to stay with a job until it was completed was in doubt. In subsequent responses he got the point across as forcefully as he could that a lack of persistence was not one of his problems.

Objection: Candidate insensitivity to corporate culture

INTERVIEWER: What's your opinion of the political situation in your company?

CANDIDATE: So far as I can tell, politics are very much a part of our organization, but they seem to be "normal," compared to other companies I've worked for.

INTERVIEWER: What do you mean by that?

CANDIDATE: At the lowest levels, decisions are technical, for the most part. People perform the tasks they are assigned, with very little margin for variation.

A level or so above this, people manage both other people and systems. The decisions are more complex. Politics seem to be a way to get answers—to offset the lack of certainty.

Then at the highest levels, from what I can tell, there's never sufficient data. It seems that there's a certain amount of intuition or experience-based guesswork that comes into play. People depend on people who have delivered for them in the past. At this level, political dynamics become a legitimate, organizational reality.

INTERVIEWER: How would you evaluate your political skills?

CANDIDATE: I don't think there's ever been an instance where I've lost ground because I misjudged a political situation. Based on that, I would evaluate my political skills as good.

INTERVIEWER: Then why did you accept a lateral transfer to another department?

CANDIDATE: There was no way to move ahead, so I went to another department that could use me. Friends in the department thought I was crazy at the time, because I had to be accepted by a closed group that had never been open to outsiders.

It turned out just fine, though, because when the corporation started downsizing, I survived because I had been cross-trained.

Critique: The candidate demonstrated that he was sensitive to corporate politics, practiced them within organizational norms, and was able to use them to his advantage in situations where it was appropriate to do so.

Objection: Possible lack of introspection

INTERVIEWER: What was the biggest work-related mistake you ever made?

CANDIDATE: I'm not sure I understand your question.

INTERVIEWER: Well, a "strategic" mistake would be a decision to, say, build Product A when marketing data indicated that you should have gone with Product B. A "work-related" mistake would be something involving interpersonal dealings or related say, to career management.

CANDIDATE: Okay. That would probably would be leaving my first employer. I've never been as productive or happy as I was my first 10 years in the business. Those were boom years. The sky was the limit. I left for Cranberry Yards thinking I had perfectly leveraged my previous experience. I was dead wrong, but I didn't realize it until it was too late.

INTERVIEWER: What do you wish you had done differently?

CANDIDATE: Thought things through more thoroughly. It was a "youth mistake" that I'd never make again.

INTERVIEWER: From the same personal perspective, what would you consider your biggest shortcoming?

CANDIDATE: Probably wanting to do things too quickly. I have a very good grasp of business issues. What I have to get better at is in waiting to make decisions until all of the data are in.

To lead others successfully, you have to commit yourself to the corporate mission—where there is one—and let all of your decisions flow from it. "Because I think it's right" is not a reason for action that wins either management approval or support from those who work for you.

INTERVIEWER: If we were to ask some business associates who know you well, how would they answer these same two questions about you?

CANDIDATE: Probably the same way. That by working to listen better and analyze more completely, I have the potential to balance two traits not often found in the same person: the ability to plan thoroughly and to implement effectively.

INTERVIEWER: What areas would they say are still in need of improvement?

CANDIDATE: I'm trying to cure myself of the belief that sooner is better than perfect. I fully realize that there are some people who still feel I don't staff my decisions long enough.

Critique: Once the candidate saw what the interviewer was up to, he fielded her questions well. More importantly, he avoided the kind of non-answer recommended by some interview advice-givers regarding questions about weaknesses, such as: "I just tried to do too much." Such answers fool no one and are patently disingenuous. Our candidate indeed has a weakness. In the past, it has affected his performance. But he has made tangible progress, and is a better worker for it. This comes through.

Objection: Candidate does not learn from his mistakes

INTERVIEWER: What weaknesses did you learn about yourself in your most recent performance review?

CANDIDATE: That I'm not clear enough about what I expect from my people when making new project assignments, or in giving them corrective feedback.

INTERVIEWER: Well, I think a lot of us fall into that category.

CANDIDATE: Well, maybe, but I wanted to do something about it.

INTERVIEWER: And what did you do?

CANDIDATE: I normally hold a staff meeting once a month. I brought up the boss's observation as an item of business. I told them I wanted to do a better job getting across what needed to be accomplished, as well as identifying behaviors and procedures that needed to be improved.

I told them that rather than discuss it further then, that I would meet with each of them for five or ten minutes over the next two weeks to hear any ideas they might have about my doing a better job. I gave them the alternative of putting their suggestions on paper and submitting them anonymously to avoid any suggestion that they were being put on the spot.

INTERVIEWER: What happened then?

CANDIDATE: I received good suggestions both at the one-on-one meetings and on paper. I then reported to them what things were going to be done differently, and asked for feedback. Everyone was happy with the results.

INTERVIEWER: So how is it working?

CANDIDATE: Occasionally, I find myself slipping back into my old ways. Fortunately, the system we put together works and keeps me from making the mistakes that used to get the department into trouble.

Critique: The candidate was honest in describing a real problem that was adversely affecting department performance. Not only did he address it forcefully, he was not reluctant to use his entire department in forging a solution, displaying enough self-confidence to accept constructive criticism from his subordinates.

Objection: Candidate lacking latest management techniques

INTERVIEWER: What examples of innovation can you point to in your management of production activities?

CANDIDATE: There were never any complaints about our operation, but last fall our management council sent several of us to observe factories in Ohio that had successfully used "continuous improvement" techniques. We were encouraged to introduce them to any extent feasible.

INTERVIEWER: How is that working out?

CANDIDATE: Previously, our Monday morning production meetings focused on current problems out in the factory: How to break up a log jam; how to gain two weeks' production time on a project that had fallen behind plan.

Now that's all changed. We realized we were making product for four types of customers. We also realized that even though all projects pass through the same seven production steps, there are four basic variations of that process, depending on which customer group we were aiming at.

INTERVIEWER: Tell me about the operational implications.

CANDIDATE: We established four customer group production teams. Membership includes those individuals key to the production of product for that group—so more people are involved. Each group meets regularly once a week to deal with their operational issues. I don't attend those meetings unless I'm asked to.

INTERVIEWER: Who handles the specifics?

CANDIDATE: My seven direct reports now meet to deal with those issues forwarded to us by the production teams. These are usually policy and planning issues that have impact across several teams, such as safety and the preventive maintenance schedule, or issues that deal with long-range questions, such as plant expansion.

Critique: The candidate, knowing that managerial techniques were a key part of the job description, made sure that he demonstrated mastery of techniques already adopted by the hiring company. He went into enough detail to convince the interviewer that (1) he was thoroughly familiar with the process; and (2) he had used it himself extensively and was comfortable administering its principles with his department. A similar example follows.

Objection: Candidate lacks innovative management skills

INTERVIEWER: What's the most significant thing you've learned in the past year?

CANDIDATE: How to recruit a team member.

INTERVIEWER: How is that different from recruiting an employee from the outside?

CANDIDATE: Actually, recruiting for a team member is a little more complex. Normally, you select the most qualified person with whom you will get along best. But a new team member's ability to get along with the other team members is as important as the candidate's ability to get along personally with the leader—maybe more so.

INTERVIEWER: So how does this tie in with the most important thing you've learned over the past year?

CANDIDATE: Well, I selected an internal candidate to fill an opening on the team. He was super-qualified, and he and I hit it off beautifully. But he threw off the rest of the team by coming on too strong. We talked about this extensively, but he was unable to make appropriate adjustments. After three months I thanked him for the effort and replaced him with someone who was a better fit.

Objection: Candidate lacks analytic planning ability

INTERVIEWER: What is the most complex planning analysis you have ever had to make?

CANDIDATE: When I was working with a major government contractor, I had to prepare business plans with five- and ten-year projections. This is difficult because Congress is the funding source, and all of its appropriations are on an annual basis. Some of the programs for which I was responsible had a five-year invention period before we could start manufacturing and deploying the product, building inventory, and training people to use it.

INTERVIEWER: How did you go about building your plan?

CANDIDATE: By collecting as much data as possible from those ordering the product—that is, the generals, admirals, and members of Congress directly involved in approving the authorizations.

We used a lot of statistical data about general economic conditions and the availability of the technical people required. For example, I had to estimate whether we had the technical ability in-house to create this product. If not, how could we procure it: for example, through a joint venture with another vendor or by employing the talent ourselves?

We also used probabilities. For example, if there was only a 10 percent chance of a certain program happening, and there were four contractors involved in the bidding, our chances of seeing any money were $2^1/2$ percent. At those odds it was very difficult to convince management it was worth the risk of investing any more time in the project.

INTERVIEWER: How effective was your planning? What were the results?

CANDIDATE: Every product we convinced management to bid on, we won. When we won, we were profitable.

Critique: From an interviewer question early in their meeting, the candidate realized that being able to handle complex problems well was one of the position's key requirements. He made sure that in every response he emphasized his analytic background and skills, and the extent to which they had contributed to his considerable success.

Objection: Lack of capacity for risk-taking

INTERVIEWER: What's the greatest business risk you've ever taken?

CANDIDATE: Going into business on my own.

INTERVIEWER: What prompted you to take that risk?

CANDIDATE: The certain knowledge that we had a product nobody else had, and that there was a market need for it.

INTERVIEWER: I see on your resume that at one point you moved your family from one coast to the other to become general manager of a new company, even though you had put in six good years with your previous employer. Wasn't that a greater risk?

CANDIDATE: In the sense that I was uprooting my family for a completely new environment it was risky, but everybody was behind the decision. We all looked upon it as an adventure.

Going into business for myself, on the other hand, required creating a new company, which in turn required capital that we had to borrow. I felt a personal responsibility for paying back the money—even though I wasn't personally liable for it— which made this a much bigger business risk.

INTERVIEWER: What was the greatest risk you did *not* take in your business life?

CANDIDATE: (pauses) I really can't think of any.

INTERVIEWER: What's your attitude toward risk?

CANDIDATE: When I'm 75, sitting in my rocker on the back porch,

I don't want to count up the "might-have-beens" and "if-only's." I realize that thinking this way puts more stress in my life. On the other hand, it gives me the opportunity to accomplish things that some people only dream about.

Critique: The candidate took a risk discussing his background in terms that indicated a willingness to live his professional life "on the edge." It was consistent with his personal philosophy, however, and he lost nothing by his candor. If the interviewer had been looking for an individual less inclined to risk and the candidate, realizing this, had answered more conservatively, both would have been done a disservice.

Objection: Lack of specialized technical experience

(These three paragraphs of a letter written to overcome the above objection are a part of the interview follow-up letter strategy introduced earlier.)

"At Machoughton, we developed print material with bar codes to allow random access for a number of Encyclopedia Vesuvio videodiscs. I convinced EV to put together a package that addressed existing instructional goals and managed the team that produced it. It is profitable and now in its third printing.

"I am the first to admit that I am not a technology genius. I am a developer of language arts instructional material. But frankly, I think the problem with most current educational technology is that it serves the needs of the medium rather than the needs of the classroom teacher or the curriculum. Over the past 10 years teachers have been sold a lot of computerized workbooks, and as a result they have developed a healthy skepticism about instructional technology.

"I'll give you a call next Tuesday at 9:00 a.m. (unless you call me to set another time), to see if this letter overcomes the concern you expressed this morning about my technical experience.

Sincerely,"

Critique: By being sure of the objection before he left the interview, the candidate was able to (1) take enough time to compose a powerful defense of his ability to do the job—and yet get the letter off the same day he interviewed; (2) acknowledge his lack of a deep expertise in the larger issue at stake; and (3) take the initiative in finding out if his defense was successful by arranging to discuss it at a specific time and date.

WRAPPING UP THE INTERVIEW

If you face no objections not already covered in Chapter 4, and foresee no problem situations of the kind covered in Chapter 5, you are ready to maximize your chances of getting a job offer—or at least a second interview. The three ways to do this:

- Restating the reasons you believe you are the ideal candidate
- Reaffirming your interest in the job
- Asking where you stand in terms of the other candidates

are covered thoroughly in Chapter 6. Your other two important post-interview chores—evaluating your interview performance and writing an interview follow-up letter—are also discussed in Chapter 6.

ANTICIPATING OBJECTIONS FOR FOLLOW-UP INTERVIEWS

Unfortunately, you won't fully appreciate our advice about the importance of fact-finding in the first interview until you get a call scheduling the second interview. At that time you will either frantically try to recall the most important problems you'd be asked to solve or calmly review your notes (some taken during the meeting; some immediately afterward) to line up the points that yet need to be made to see if you and the job are a good match.

Being invited back for a second interview means that you are f the finalists for the job—or at least one of the semifinalists. your best job from here on requires continued preparation. me you go in to the next interview with both assets and f your questioning has been sharp, your listening acute, and your notes complete, you have almost as good a picture of these assets and liabilities as does your interviewer—who will be referring to her own notes. Go through your Assets and Liabilities checklist to help you prepare for the next interview.

ADDITIONAL READING

Fry, Ronald W. *101 Great Answers to the Toughest Interview Questions.* Hawthorne, NJ: Career Press, 1991. Preparation and practice—the only way to go to eliminate the anxieties associated with employment interviews.

Nirenberg, Jesse S. *How to Sell Your Ideas.* New York: McGraw-Hill, 1984. Pragmatic approach to interpersonal communication and persuading others to accept your ideas.

Wilson, Robert F. *Interview to Win.* (Videotape; 32 min., color.) New Haven, CT: Wilson McLeran, Inc., 1992. Before and after mock interviews provide insight in identifying and overcoming objections. "A wonderful choice . . . excellent addition to all career development collections." *The Library Journal.*

Yate, Martin J. *Knock 'Em Dead With Great Answers to Tough Interview Questions.* Boston: Bob Adams, Inc., 1991. How to handle objections, illegal questions, and interviews in unconventional settings.

5

Overcoming Camouflaged Objections

Many interview objections are difficult to identify, primarily because they are not what they seem to be. In this chapter we will help you recognize and deal with substantive objections disguised in more euphemistic form.

Camouflaged objections are usually the result of questions the interviewer thought of but did not ask (described in Chapter 4). Such judgments made about a candidate usually are based on assumption or a combination of other subjective mindsets.

Often the objection results from questions the interviewer cannot legally ask without running afoul of equal employment opportunity regulations. Obviously, if the questions are not asked, the employer is less likely to be accused of prejudicial hiring practices. Your job—not an easy one—is to peel away the layers of doubt standing in the way of your employment (and the resulting apparent risk to the employer), whatever the cause of the uneasiness.

For this reason, in the case of camouflaged objections, there will be one step in the resolution process that must be dealt with before going through the steps described in Chapter 4. We'll call this "Smoking out the objection."

For the rest of this chapter we'll attempt to identify camouflaged objections in a number of areas, then help you devise interview strategies to:

- Smoke out the objection
- Acknowledge the objection
- Neutralize the objection

Your job is to relieve an interviewer's anxiety; to alter what may be an erroneous perception. But this must be done in a way that addresses the employer's concerns at the expense of your own. Any attempt to simply debate the validity of the objection with your interviewer will be both futile and counterproductive.

Keep in mind that the examples we use—both in this chapter and in earlier chapters—include both actual and hypothetical situations. The script is intended to lay out the strategy for neutralizing each objection in a realistic way *for the specific set of circumstances described*, not provide dialogue that will necessarily mirror your situation. (For real-life case studies of job seekers who have successfully overcome various kinds of objections, see Appendix B. These success stories come from our files and from those of other career counselors. In some instances we have included the subject's resume, disguised, to give you a more complete picture of the problem situation and how it was overcome.)

There is no way of predicting, obviously, how an interviewer may respond to a specific scenario. Different employers will have different agendas and perspectives. You'll be on your own and have to improvise a good part of the time. Being sure you have dealt with a situation honestly and thoroughly is the most important consideration. And much of that will have to do with the way you prepared a strategy for your particular objection.

Your best efforts to neutralize objections will not always be successful, even using all of the tools discussed in this book. We can offer you an edge over other candidates seeking the same position, though, to give you the best possible shot at the job.

SMOKING OUT CAMOUFLAGED OBJECTIONS

Some of you already know what objections you are likely to face. The problem is, if the objection is not expressed by the interviewer for whatever reason, you won't have an opportunity to counter or neutralize it. Sometimes you'll need to ask more than one probing question to dig out the reason(s) you are not being considered for the job. For most such objections, whether you find your problem listed on the following pages or not, our advice is to avoid debating the interviewer about it at all costs. Instead, neutralize it by stressing any job-related strengths that address it directly. The rest of this chapter consists of objection examples in a number of categories, with suggestions for neutralizing each.

The Equal Employment Opportunity Commission regulations discussed in Chapter 4 protect against discrimination based on age, sex, physical disability, race, color, national origin, or religion. It is in these areas that camouflaged objections are likely to hide.

Objections About Age

Age is the most common objection masquerading as something less onerous. Although employers are prohibited from discriminating against older workers, hundreds of thousands of men and women in their sixties, fifties—sometimes even in their forties—are denied employment every year.

The Age Discrimination in Employment Act protects everyone over forty, but if an employer uses another reason for rejection—if indeed a reason *is* given—there is practically no recourse. This is why the "overqualified" rejection comes in so handy as a way for employers to avoid hiring older job seekers.

The real objection is more frequently based on a fear that an older employee is more expensive to hire or will perform less ably than a younger worker—sometimes both. Some of these concerns are real; others are either imaginary or stereotypic.

One valid concern is, because an older hire will retire sooner than a younger one, less time remains for the employer to gain a return on the investment made in hiring, orienting, and training.

Advantages of Hiring Older Workers

A 1992 Conference Board study, on the other hand, found that older workers are more reliable than younger workers, have better work attitudes and job skills, are absent less often, and are less likely to quit. Similarly, a Commonwealth Fund study followed the results of a hardware chain's three-year experiment testing the performance of older workers. From 1988 to 1991 the corporation staffed one of its six stores solely with employees over 50 years old.

Among the surprising results:

- The store staffed by the older workers was about 18 percent more profitable than the other five, and nearly 9 percent more profitable than the total company average.

- The turnover rate was five times higher at stores staffed largely with younger workers.

- The ratio of sales to labor costs at the over-50s store during this period was much better than two of the other stores, and just as good as that of the remaining two.

As a result of the study, top management decided to staff two more stores with 50-plus workers only, and to drastically increase their recruitment of older candidates. It may take time for such workplace enlightenment to catch on nationwide, but for older workers there finally seem to be signs of change.

The Age Objection

In most situations it will not be in your best interests to verbalize the "age objection," or even to indicate your awareness that this might be one of the concerns your interviewer has.

Rather, if you have reason to believe your age is acting against you in the interview, defuse it for the reasons you believe your interviewer considers it an objection. Here are a few examples:

Objection: "Overqualified" (Interviewer has various doubts about candidate with 30-plus years experience)

INTERVIEWER: Well, I see that you had 14 direct reports while you were at Pharmacraft. This is a small personnel department here—it would be just the three of you—and will remain that way for the foreseeable future.

CANDIDATE: That's really of no concern to me. Those 14 people were really more than I needed for the last couple of years. Several of them were management trainees given to me as a developmental assignment. As you've described this job, I think what excites me is that you will be overhauling the compensation program fairly soon. I had a chance to work on a similar upgrading at Elgin Watch, and management was quite pleased with it.

INTERVIEWER: Well, we've got a few department heads to get on board before corporate signs off. I'm afraid not everybody is behind the idea.

CANDIDATE: That's not unusual. I ran a series of seminars laying out our objectives at Elgin, and even then had to twist a few arms before everybody came around.

INTERVIEWER: Problem is, we've got some pretty opinionated people around here. This may turn into a job and a half.

CANDIDATE: Actually, it doesn't sound like anything I haven't handled before. It is tough to stay up half the night negotiating and still show up early the next morning ready for your other jobs. For better or worse, though, that's the name of the game until you get everybody on the same page.

INTERVIEWER: That's pretty strenuous work, isn't it?

CANDIDATE: Sure, but it doesn't last forever. I'm in good health and I enjoy the process. My references will attest to it. What kind of groundwork have you laid so far?

Critique
1. The candidate's earlier questioning established that the job included additional responsibilities his experience qualified him to perform, and that he would enjoy.

2. He gave every impression that this was a job he wanted and would accept if it were offered to him.

3. When the interviewer tried to discourage him by indicating that the amount of work was possibly more than he wanted to handle and that some of the personalities involved might prove difficult, he cited his problem-solving background and exhibited continued interest.

Objection: "Overqualified" (Candidate is 58-year-old marketing vice president of a tool company, interviewing for a marketing manager's job; smaller company, same industry. Has 33 years experience, 30 of them in sales with a large computer firm.)

INTERVIEWER: Bill, let's get into it. Why don't you walk me through your background.

CANDIDATE: Well, my current assignment is very similar to your marketing position, as I understand it. When I joined Cartwright three years ago as head of marketing, I was able to build on my sales background at ACI.

INTERVIEWER: Then you're primarily a salesman.

CANDIDATE: You could say that, but I did have 10 years of sales management as well. In that role I was there to observe the rep's selling tactics, not make the close. I gave the rep developmental feedback, too—but not until we were off the client site. I think that was good background.

As marketing manager at Cartwright, my job is somewhat the same, except that I look for even more strategic issues: the customer's reaction to our basic presentation and the effectiveness of the product package and sales aids. Off site my job is to analyze the personal observations, and then implement improvements for positioning and presenting the product more effectively.

INTERVIEWER: Well, you know we're building here. It's going to be pretty crazy for a year or so. I should think that after getting things under control at Cartwright, you'd be ready to take it easy for a while. Or maybe it's the commute. You spend an hour each way, don't you? Here you'd practically be able to walk to work.

CANDIDATE: That *is* attractive, I must admit. But actually, I don't even notice the commute. I'm on the road about 60 percent of the time anyway. I spend Monday in the office, and leave directly from there for two or three days in the field, usually getting back to the office on Friday. On the way home that evening I tape my field report, which is typed over the weekend by a local secretarial service and ready for distribution on Monday morning.

Actually, it was the challenge of your expansion that got me to answer your ad. I think everything I've done up to now has prepared me for it.

Critique

1. Bill successfully defused the objection that his extensive sales background was inappropriate to the marketing position by emphasizing his ACI sales management experience, with its excellent crossover value. He also demonstrated that his current job was virtually identical to the one he was interviewing for.

2. He downplayed the vice presidency at Cartwright, as well as his numerous promotions at ACI, so as not to give the impression that the perks of officership were important to him at a smaller company.

3. Bill neutralized the implied objection that his age and possibly declining energy level might be the only reasons he wanted a job with a company closer to home by (1) describing his heavy workload and travel schedule; (2) assuring the interviewer that the challenge of the open position was attractive to him; and (3) refuting the contention that his motivation for changing jobs was a shorter commute—in general, projecting an image as an energetic, ambitious candidate.

Objections About Gender

Recent studies indicate that considerable progress has been made in the drive for parity between men and women in the workplace. From investment bankers earning six figures to sales clerks at the minimum wage level, women gained a net 18 percent on men in the 1980s, with similar prospects for the 1990s. The median annual salary for men dropped 8 percent after inflation to $28,843 from $31,315 between 1979 and 1990, while the comparable salary for women rose 10 percent during this same period, to $20,656 from $18,683.[1] As more and more states enact equal pay codes, similar gains can be expected in the 1990s.

Nevertheless, in terms of parity, a level playing field this is not.

---

[1]"Closing the Gender Gap," *Society* (March–April, 1993).

The "glass ceiling" still exists in many industries, creating an artificial compensation barrier that prevents women from making as much money as men.

Furthermore, a recent study reinforces the notion that women have higher job-turnover rates than men, but not because they are less committed to their work. According to a report in the *Journal of Organizational Behavior*, women were twice as likely as men to admit that they would "definitely" or "probably" leave their organization within two years. Nearly all were frustrated with the lack of career opportunities, largely based on discrimination, high expectations, underlying performance problems, or differential treatment in the appraisal process.

Following are three common objections women face in the interview situation:

Objection: Interviewer doubts female candidate's ability to move into managerial position

INTERVIEWER: Two promotions in four years. That's quite impressive, Ms. Obrink, considering that your lab experience was relatively limited up to that point.

CANDIDATE: Thank you. I catch on quickly, if I do say so myself.

INTERVIEWER: Here at Midland the problem is a little different. We're quite a bit larger than your operation at Carstairs, as you know, and somewhat more decentralized, as well. When our three product lines spin off in November, I'm going to have to name a new laboratory manager for each one. So everyone I hire between now and then (I have four open slots to fill) will either be leadership material or a specialist of some kind.

CANDIDATE: Well. Since I'm a generalist, I guess you're wondering how I would do as one of the lab managers. Do you have people in mind for any of these three jobs now?

INTERVIEWER: For one of them, yes. The other two are wide open.

CANDIDATE: Thanks for your candor, Mr. Marquard. I can say that—the way you've described the job—I believe I could move into one of the manager's jobs quite easily. My second promotion at Carstairs was as supervisor of a four-person research and production department. What I didn't know then about managing could fill 10 books. But I learned in a hurry, and have the job assessment reviews to prove it.

INTERVIEWER: Yes, I can see by your resume that you accomplished a great deal in 22 months. The problem is, I'm talking about a 17-person department—with more than a few high-powered guys here. No implied criticism, but if the boss isn't seen as the boss in every sense, we've got problems.

CANDIDATE: How many female managers do you have here?

INTERVIEWER: Now wait. I think I know what you're asking, and that isn't the issue here.

CANDIDATE: What I want to assure you of, Mr. Marquard, is that my gender won't affect my managerial performance in the slightest. The three men in my department at Carstairs and I all got along extremely well—and I had to lay some heavy deadlines on them for a couple of the projects we got out. I'd be happy for you to call any of them for a reference.

INTERVIEWER: I'm delighted to hear it, and I didn't mean to imply that your work would be any less effective than that of the men who manage here.

Critique
1. Ms. Obrink guessed early in the interview that another agenda might be affecting the hiring process. She realized she might be wrong, but felt she needed to deal with her perception head-on, rather than leave it to chance.

2. Her direct question about the number of female managers at Midland forced Mr. Marquard to deal with the topic, at the obvious risk of putting him on the defensive, but without which she would never have known.

3. She was able to handle Mr. Marquard's response in a way that defused any possible downside he might feel in hiring a female lab manager, and at the same time reinforcing her "genderless" qualifications for the job.

In some instances, your best recourse is to volunteer a statement concerning the objection as soon as you realize that it might be a real problem.

Objection: Interviewer thinks married female candidate's job tenure will be affected sometime in the future by probable parenting duties

INTERVIEWER: Well, I guess that covers everything I had. Are there any other questions you have?

CANDIDATE: There is one thing. Since the territory for this job is four states—with all the time away from home *that* implies— let me address a question you might be too polite to ask.

I am married, as you know. Bill and I have decided not to have children until we've paid back all of our education loans. That will take a little over five years. He's a dentist, and will be establishing his practice here in town. So I am looking for an employer for the long haul. I would like to travel now while I am most able to, maybe work part-time when the kids are small, and then fulltime again when they go to school.

Critique Knowing that the interviewer was unlikely to initiate this topic, the candidate left nothing to chance. She volunteered enough information to neutralize the inferred objection. (A similar objection faced by married women with children is that child-care will interfere with job attendance and performance. This can be similarly defused by sharing with the interviewer any arrangements that have been made to the extent that it becomes a non-issue.)

Objections About Physical Disability[2]

Five out of every six people with a disability acquired it later in life, rather than at birth. So even though none of us can do much about

---

[2]Tens of thousands of individuals in this country have minor mental or emotional disorders not severe enough to keep them from qualifying for certain kinds of work. If you have such a friend or relative who wants to work for pay, call the local office of your state or federal Health & Human Services department for procedural advice.

our age, race, or gender, any of us could be searching for a job with the additional liability of a disability—at any time.

This fact does nothing to relieve most employers' reluctance to hire a person with a disability, unfortunately—that reluctance, in turn, is based almost entirely on a fear of the unknown.

Part of the problem has to do with a preconception—often erroneous—about what specific duties people with various kinds of physical limitations can and cannot perform. The other part is in dealing with the discomfort felt by an interviewer for whom meeting a disabled person may be a new experience.

The EEOC has done a good job at both federal and state levels of protecting the rights of anyone who falls under its definition of "disabled." Nevertheless, it is impossible to legislate against *camouflaged* objections. Neutralizing these objections—after identifying and acknowledging them—can be accomplished *only* by hard work and diligence on the part of the interviewee.

As with age- and sex-related camouflaged objections, most important is to put the interviewer at ease, so as to begin to focus as quickly as possible on one's suitability for the job.

Tom Widney, an electronics engineer from Albuquerque who has spent the past 22 years in a wheelchair, says the secret is to first come to terms with, and then be comfortable with, one's own disability.

"This way you're able to emphasize your attributes as they apply to the challenges of the job," says Widney. "I often say that I've had lots of practice finding practical solutions to problems I face in my environment. If I get this idea across, it is easier for the employer to focus on my abilities, rather than on my disability."

If your disability is recent enough so that bitterness is still a part of your life, better wait to job hunt until you have more perspective on your situation. Any lingering emotional effects surrounding your disability will certainly affect your interview performance and provide only negative reinforcement.

Here are a few additional ways Tom Widney tries to overcome any camouflaged objections about his disability. He emphasizes that his methods may not be appropriate for everyone, but that they have worked for him:

- If the interviewer doesn't bring up the disability, don't you bring it up.

- Focus on your attributes and emphasize them. (Basically, you are relating to an individual for whom meeting a person with a disability may be a new experience.)
- When you meet interviewers for the first time, give them all the clues they need for relating well to you.
- Don't even *hint* that you "deserve" the job.
- Sell, sell, sell your abilities.

In the event that your disability is discussed in the interview and is not camouflaged, here are some statistics you should be aware of. They were taken from a 1987 Lou Harris survey for the International Center for the Disabled and deal with companies that hired disabled employees:

- 3/4 of all managers said that the average cost of employing a person with disabilities was about the same as the cost of hiring someone without disabilities.
- 8 out of 10 line managers said disabled employees were no harder to supervise or support than were employees with no obvious disabilities.
- 39 percent of all line managers rated disabled employees as better than employees with no disabilities in such areas as willingness to work hard, reliability, attendance, and punctuality.
- 27 percent of all department heads and line managers rated their disabled employees' performance as *excellent*; 64 percent rated it as *good*; 3 percent rated it as *fair*; and none rated it as *poor*.

The enforcement of EEOC regulations and a gradual shift in attitude toward handicapped workers are causing more and more companies to invest in applicable training programs and adjustments in workplace equipment.

According to a *Harvard Business Review* report on recent technology for the blind, "machines can read a printed page out loud, using synthetic speech, or receive typed input and produce braille output; devices . . . attached to a computer terminal will speak whatever material appears on screen; and systems can read written matter onto a disk then output it in braille, synthetic speech, or large print."

If you are unsure as to whether a solution exists for a problem you have, call the Job Accommodation Network, with offices at the University of West Virginia in Morgantown, WV. Their phone number is 1-800-526-7234.

Objection Employer doubts ability of disabled job seeker to fit into the company Scheme of Things and justify a long-term investment if hired on a full-time, permanent basis

INTERVIEWER: How would you be getting to work?

CANDIDATE: I have a car.

INTERVIEWER: You drive, then.

CANDIDATE: Oh, yes. And I have a license in good standing.

[For other situations, simply speak in as much detail as is called for about the thoroughness with which you have solved your problem, whether through public transportation, car pool, regular assistance from relatives or friends, etc.]

INTERVIEWER: Well, I want to thank you for coming in. I think you are an excellent candidate, and we'll certainly be getting back to you.

CANDIDATE: Thank you. I realize that it's a big commitment to hire someone these days. Let me make a suggestion that will greatly reduce the risk for you regarding any doubts you may have about my ability to do the job. I would gladly start on a temporary basis, and in two or three months—whatever you were comfortable with—we could review the situation. If at that time you were not satisfied with the quality or quantity of my work, we would simply shake hands and I would move on. If you liked what I was doing, we could discuss a long-term agreement.

Critique
1. Before the interview the candidate researched the company to learn what special accommodations might have to be made, if any, to hire him. He was ready to address any that might come up and probe to smoke out any objections the interviewer had but was reluctant to bring up herself.
2. At every opportunity the candidate seeks to reassure the employer, both implicitly and explicitly, that bringing him

on board will be an asset to the company, not a favor to the job seeker. Tom Widney, previously quoted, says that he tries to get across the fact that his disability itself has taught him "'books' about practical problem solving. I try to 'screech' my talents and how I would use them to benefit the company, far in excess of whatever accommodation it might have to make for me."

3. If he senses no job offer forthcoming, the candidate has nothing to lose by offering his services for a finite period of time. It indicates his willingness to take a risk, while at the same time sharply reducing the employer's risk. Offering to sign any reasonable agreement the employer draws up will further diminish the company's risk.

Objections About Race, Color, and Nationality

Some of you who have lost job offers because you are black or Hispanic may have difficulty believing that this situation is changing slowly for the better. Employers who make hiring decisions for these and other non-job-related reasons have been with us for a long while, and unfortunately will be around for some time to come.

Objections based on race, color, and nationality are almost universally camouflaged, because they are racist. Few would admit that racism is the real reason for rejection, however. Even fewer would deny that racism had any part to play in their hiring decisions—and believe it.

"Business has always been inherently conservative," writes Andrew Hacker in *Two Nations: Black and White, Separate, Hostile, Unequal.* " . . . Hence the tendency to play it safe, which usually means hiring as white a workforce as possible. There is also the worry that blacks who are promoted to supervisory positions may not obtain the best performance from white subordinates, who may be resentful if not actually resistant. Chief executives may smile wanly and agree that the problem is one of prejudice. Not their own, of course, but that of customers and others who still cling to stereotypes."

Such prejudice extends to Asians and Hispanics as well, to be sure, and is not restricted just to blacks. For this reason some nonwhites have opted out of the white-dominated work force, choosing instead to work in less stressful environments with people more like themselves.

Obviously this is not an option open to many. To earn a livelihood, many non-white job seekers have no choice but to look to mainstream opportunities, even though their prospects are limited. In his chapter "Being Black in America," Andrew Hacker writes in *Two Nations*, "Even after playing by the rules, you find yourself hitting a not-so-invisible ceiling. You wonder if you are simply corporate wallpaper, a protective coloration they find it prudent to display. You begin to suspect that a 'qualification' you will always lack is white pigmentation."

So for those of you ready, willing, and able to fight the odds as well as the system, the advice is simple: Leave nothing to chance. Insofar as you can, match your diction, dress, and appearance with that of the corporate culture you observe. Bring up aspects of your life that you and the interview may have in common: a shared interest or hobby, for example. "You have to convince that person that you're OK and will fit in," says H. Lance Barkley, Vice President of Human Resources at the National Geographic Society.

Ask a "mainstream" friend or acquaintance to test you. You need to lose as much of any accent as you can, and be sure your clothes and appearance fall within conventional norms. Give the interviewer nothing to use against you, nothing to distract her from the message you are trying to convey: I can do whatever is asked of me, and I will fit in easily.

This is your job: to increase your chances of *getting* the job. (Also read Appendix A: "Thinker, Visionary, Driver, Friend—Four Interviewer Personalities.")

Objection   Limited English proficiency (Candidate with pronounced accent is judged to be deficient in other aspects of the language)

CANDIDATE: There was an interesting article in the business section of yesterday's *Observer* about the new microchip produced by a consortium of computer manufacturers.

INTERVIEWER: Really? What did it say?

CANDIDATE: The profile of the fellow who put the consortium together was fascinating, but it didn't go much beyond that.

Actually, a story in last month's *Byte* magazine went into more detail about why the new chip is better and described the engineering that made it possible.

Critique The candidate demonstrated that his technological knowledge was not impeded by continuing to learn in his second language, and that he was interested enough in mastering English to regularly read mainstream periodicals.

Miscellaneous Camouflaged Objections

Some of the following situations may be applicable to your situation. Adapt them as necessary:

Objection Difficulty of adapting to new industry

CANDIDATE: When I look back over my 15 years in sales, I realize that what I did best and enjoyed most was researching and launching new products. I gladly did those things most salesmen hate: competitive analysis, product specifications, analyzing test market data, developing rollout plans, pricing research, commission schedules, budgets, internal presentations, and sales training.

I now see that I was my boss's marketing expert, even though he never recognized me as such because ours was considered a very strong "sales company." What that meant was that they believed in modest base salaries and very generous commissions.

For me to make a good living doing what I do best, though, it's time for me to move on to a company that values the marketing area more appropriately.

Critique The candidate tried to show his thorough knowledge of marketing function nitty-gritty, to make the interviewer comfortable with his ability to make a smooth transition to an unfamiliar industry.

Objection Difficulty of adapting to new function

CANDIDATE: I guess I've been gravitating toward sales throughout my career. Sure enough, I started as a programmer. My first big promotion came when I was asked to write systems specifications for product ideas submitted by marketing and sales. The next big opportunity was to be promoted to technical rep and start to work directly for the customers. So, you can see this has been a developmental migration rather than a sudden change of direction.

Critique   Most important to the candidate was to increase the interviewer's comfort level with his projected effectiveness in sales by enumerating all of the sales-related jobs he had held while actually working in another function.

Objection   Difficulty adapting from smaller to larger company

CANDIDATE: Starting in a small company, I was exposed to more varied situations faster and was given more responsibility sooner than I might have in a large corporate-management development program. From my first day on the job the executives knew me by first name. They knew about my every success and misstep. I learned early about pressure. As one of my bosses said, "Every time you make a mistake, it's my money you're washing down the drain."

Critique   The candidate emphasizes that he will bring to the larger company a familiarity with the problems of others in a variety of functions, and so be a more valuable employee. He is no stranger to pressure, which many large-company officials feel is mainly a function of size.

Objection   Difficulty adapting from larger to smaller company

CANDIDATE: Grand Central Roach Control *was* a big organization, comprised of many small, independent operating units. Their strategy was to foster entrepreneurship by minimizing interference and direction from above. In this sense, my division (which was about the size of your firm) was very similar to a small company in its structure and decision-making capability.

Critique   The answer is to find commonalities between the two different work experiences in order to indicate to the interviewer that any adjustment will be minimal.

Objection   Difficulty adapting to different corporate culture

CANDIDATE: Every organization has its own way of conducting its business. Having worked successfully in a number of different organizations, I have learned to be very adaptable. I have no one fixed method of operation that I superimpose on others. Rather, I blend in, observe what works, and when it is appropriate to suggest an improvement, do so incrementally so as not to disrupt the natural flow of things.

Critique   The candidate is interested in the good of the company at the expense of his personal ambition, all documented by his work record.

Objection   Job-jumper: may be more interested in learning the latest technology than staying with the work at hand

CANDIDATE: When I decided that computers were going to be my livelihood, I realized I needed to move around after college to gain experience in different operating environments.

INTERVIEWER: Excuse me, but four jobs in the past eight years?

CANDIDATE: I hear what you're saying, but if I had joined a major company at the outset, my assignments would have become increasingly complex, but they would all have been on the same hardware—or very similar software. If this were a major city, I could have joined a consulting company, and they would have kept me hopping.

INTERVIEWER: So what was your rationale?

CANDIDATE: I chose to keep growing by changing companies. Unorthodox, I know, but I thought at the time that this was the only way. I want to complete the "journeyman" phase of my career and assume some kind of leadership position that will allow my employer and me to get a fair, long-term return on all the solid experience I have accumulated.

Critique   The candidate presents a reasoned rationale for the four jobs he held in eight years. For some of you it will be less easy. Refer to the advice offered for neutralizing the loss of a recent job in Chapters 2 and 4. The problems may be similar, even though you left all of your previous jobs voluntarily.

Objection   A reference check (See Chapter 6) indicates a possible candidate with an attitude problem

INTERVIEWER: Of the employers for whom you have worked, which did you like the least, and why?

CANDIDATE: That's a difficult question. My past employers have been quite varied—and I interpret that to include supervisors, as well, because there are many more of them to pick from.

INTERVIEWER: Sure. Supervisors as well.

CANDIDATE: All of them had effective and ineffective features. I learned something from all of them. The ones I liked best were those with whom I grew the most.

INTERVIEWER: How about a specific?

CANDIDATE: Well, there was Carl Weinstein at Kane County Regulator. He was a "roman candle" of ideas. Rarely did he ever tell me that I had to complete a project in a prescribed way. Rather, he delegated the entire process to me: not only the best method of completing it, but how to allocate my time and resources.

INTERVIEWER: Tell me about one.

CANDIDATE: Carl once said we needed a better way of tracking our customer contracts. He had in mind using the word processor for storing the typed contracts alphabetically by account name.

I thought of using the computer instead of the word processor, so that in addition to our current contracts, we could create a profile on each customer, as well as a billing and payment history. We could generate mailing lists sorted by zip code or requirements we were not yet contracted to serve.

Carl loved it, and gave me the go-ahead. It worked out great.

INTERVIEWER: Which bosses have you liked least?

CANDIDATE: Those who've been least demanding. Not to mention any names, I once worked in a company that functioned more like a government bureaucracy. My boss was more concerned that I do things the way they had been done, rather than looking for ways to do things better.

INTERVIEWER: In terms of corporate culture, where have you been least productive?

CANDIDATE: Where people don't give challenging assignments. Where people won't delegate, I can't operate.

Critique The candidate was not trapped by the interviewer's line of questioning, designed to encourage negative responses wherever possible. Instead he gave unsatisfactory bosses the benefit of the doubt, but without compromising his honesty and without personalizing his criticism. His detailed descriptions were restricted to positive experiences.

Anticipating Objections

If you are absolutely certain your candidacy is down the tubes for whatever reason, you have nothing to lose by bringing up the camouflaged objection yourself—in as nonthreatening a way as possible.

Depending on the way the conversation is going, your best bet will probably be to wait until all of your "indirect defusing" tactics are exhausted; then bring up the objection you sense is on the interviewer's mind. Here are a few sample introductory phrases:

> "You've asked a lot of questions about my background. Now there's one point I'd like to bring up . . ."

or,

> "I get the feeling there's something bothering you about my candidacy. I may be dead wrong, but . . ."

or,

> "Can you help me with something? I'm getting a strong impression that you think . . ."

Stylistic Objections

In many of the objections laid out in this chapter, the candidate's comments are printed in their entirety, without "stage directions." In point of fact, what you say and how you say it will have a lot to do with the way the interviewer responds to you. You may need to change your course, depending on a question you get in mid-presentation.

Some interviewer objections, in fact, have less to do with content than they do with style. A well-prepared candidate can be so intent on getting his message across that he tends to blurt out an entire stage of his background without checking the interviewer's expressions or body language to see how the message is being received. Following is an interview section modulated to allow the interviewer to break in periodically to adjust the direction of the questioning:

INTERVIEWER: So, please tell me about your assignment with Worldwide Petroleum.

CANDIDATE: Well, it started as a management traineeship while I was in graduate school.

INTERVIEWER: How were you selected?

CANDIDATE: Five of us were chosen on the basis of our interest in the industry and our class standing . . .

INTERVIEWER: Which was . . . ?

CANDIDATE: Upper 20 percent. I graduated with honors.

INTERVIEWER: So what about the traineeship?

CANDIDATE: Worldwide sent me to Australia the semester between my first and second year . . .

INTERVIEWER: (Nods.)

CANDIDATE: I was assigned to the cost control department and helped implement a less expensive method of distributing product throughout Australia using a computer program supplied by Worldwide headquarters.

INTERVIEWER: Can you program?

CANDIDATE: Yes, to a limited degree in COBOL.

INTERVIEWER: Ok. Go on.

CANDIDATE: We worked out an arrangement whereby call orders came into a central clearing house, and they decided which product would be distributed from which storage facility on which truck.

INTERVIEWER: (Nods.) Um hmm.

CANDIDATE: Previously, all orders and dispatching were handled regionally.

INTERVIEWER: (Nods.)

CANDIDATE: Upon graduation I started fulltime with Worldwide.

INTERVIEWER: Ok, let's skip ahead to your current assignment.

Critique   The candidate was sensitive to the interviewer's reaction to his presentation, and made sure he was continuing to provide information the interviewer seemed to want, by pausing at the end of each complete thought to gauge the interviewer's response.

ADJUSTING YOUR STYLE TO THE INTERVIEWER

Your own objections may not have been dealt with in Chapters 4 and 5. (We welcome your letters to tell us of additional objections you think should be covered in the Second Edition of *Conquer Interview Objections*—or ways of overcoming objections that weren't covered here but that worked for you.) In general, your best advice is to prepare for the interview as well as you can—in terms of both the employer's requirements and the possible liabilities that may diminish your chances of getting a job offer.

Imagine you are the person who will interview you in several days, whether it be an executive recruiter, the hiring manager, or a human resource manager. Write down all of the questions *you* would ask you, as well as the answers most likely to neutralize your interviewer's objections. Practice your answers until you are comfortable with them.

Now write down all of the questions you hope you don't get asked and write down answers to *them*. Similarly rehearse your answers with a friend who knows you professionally, to be sure of their completeness and authenticity.

When Harrington "Duke" Drake, former CEO of The Dun & Bradstreet Corporation, faced an interview by a reporter or met with a group outside the corporation, he asked key staff members to compile a list of all possible hostile questions, along with suggested answers. Then he and his colleagues rehearsed the Q. and A. session until all responses were perfect. When asked how he discovered this tactic, Drake said, "I think it's because I came up through sales."

ADDITIONAL READING

Bolles, Richard N. *Job-Hunting Tips for the So-Called Handicapped or People Who Have Disabilities*. Berkeley, CA: Ten Speed Press, 1991. Explores the reasons behind employers' reactions to disabled persons. Upbeat, practical suggestions for changing these reactions.

Hacker, Andrew. *Two Nations: Black and White, Separate, Hostile, Unequal*. New York: Charles Scribner's Sons, 1992. Startling analysis of a divided society, depicting realities of family life, income distribution, and employment, as well as current controversies affecting education and politics.

Joel, Lewin G. III. *Every Employee's Guide to the Law*. New York: Pantheon Books, 1993. The front-cover blurb says it all: Everything you need to know about your rights in the workplace—and what to do if they are violated.

Ray, Samuel N. *Job Hunting After 50: Strategy for Success*. New York: John Wiley & Sons, 1991. How to display your skills, knowledge, and experience in ways that will make employers see beyond age objections to the real issue: your value to the organization.

Swain, Madeleine and Robert. *Out of the Organization: How Fast Could You Find a Job?* New York: Mastermedia Ltd, 1988. See Chapter 6, "Gender Is More Than a Six-Letter Word," for a useful discussion of tactics when women are either interviewed by men or are interviewing them.

6

Making the Close; Negotiating Compensation

At some point you will have worked your way through all of the screening interviews and find yourself in the "selection interview." Whether this is the first interview or the ninth, it's where the decision to hire will be made.

The job may be yours to lose (meaning they've decided either to hire you or to start the process anew), or you could be in tight competition with one or more other candidates.

Knowing which of these situations applies to you is useful information to have. It is also a continuation of what sales trainers call the "closing process"—as in "closing the deal." If you've been using the suggestions provided in previous chapters, you've been closing all along.

Every question you ask in your screening interviews is designed to move the process along—to get you closer to a job offer; to help you decide if this is the job for you. In other words, to help you *close*.

In Chapter 2 you closed by asking questions that clarified issues and illuminated possible problem areas that might arise in the first minutes of your interview.

In Chapter 3, all of your positioning questions moved the hiring process closer to a decision point by: (1) more precisely defining the requirements of the job; and (2) determining how well you presented yourself as a solution to the problems identified.

In Chapters 4 and 5, which dealt with various types of objections to your candidacy, all of the questions were intended to clarify and sharpen the focus on the central issues:

- Is this the right job for me?
- Am I the right person for the job?

There are several remaining steps in the interview end-game that you should master in order to maximize your chances of success.

WRAPPING UP THE INTERVIEW

After making every effort to eliminate the objections to your candidacy, you need to maximize your chances of getting a job offer—or at least a second interview. You do this by:

- Restating the reasons you believe you are the ideal candidate
- Reaffirming your interest in the job
- Asking where you stand in terms of the other candidates

Restate Your Qualifications

If there has been no opportunity during the interview for you to state your cumulative, job-related qualifications at one time, this is it. Or, if you can improve on your presentation now that you have a more complete picture of the job, this may be your last face-to-face opportunity.

Other than this, a total recitation of how good you think you are may be a counter-productive way to finish the interview. Make this extremely subjective decision based on your gut feeling for your total interview performance.

If you sense a reservation to your candidacy on the part of the interviewer, offer to submit something in writing that may change the interviewer's mind. For example:

CANDIDATE: If there's anything I can do to convince you that I should stay at the top of your list, just let me know. If you consider some aspect of my background less than ideal, for example, I'd be happy to address it with a trial assignment, perhaps, or anything else that might be appropriate.

INTERVIEWER: Interesting idea. Let me think about it; I may be getting back to you.

Reaffirm Your Interest in the Job

Many candidates assume that because they show up for the interview, no further evidence is necessary that they want the job. Don't assume anything. Given two candidates of relatively equal merit, a hiring executive will invariably offer the job to the person most interested in doing it—or who *appears* to be. Here is an aggressive close that may be appropriate for you at some point:

CANDIDATE: I don't want to appear too pushy. It's just that I know the job is right for me, and I want you to view me as a serious, capable candidate.

INTERVIEWER: Well, that I do, believe me. Thanks for coming in.

CANDIDATE: My pleasure. Thanks for your time.

Ask Where You Stand with the Other Candidates

This is very important. You won't come across as nosy by asking about the hiring process. This is information you need to help plan your post-interview strategy. If you are among the first to be interviewed, you will need patience; if you are among the last, you must act with a greater sense of urgency. Consider the following sequence:

CANDIDATE: One last thing: What is your timing in coming to a decision to hire?

INTERVIEWER: Well, let's see. I have four more candidates to see before we decide whom to bring in for the second time.

CANDIDATE: Have you made up your mind yet whether I'll be one of those to make the first cut?

INTERVIEWER: Difficult to say. I should know by Friday—Monday latest.

EVALUATING YOUR INTERVIEW PERFORMANCE

Immediately after you leave your interviewer's office, you have two important jobs to complete. First is to evaluate your interview performance as honestly as you can. You need to make a list of all of those areas you handled well and those in which you could have done better. This list and the interpretation you draw from it will be crucial in preparing both your follow-up letter and your strategy for subsequent interviews, should you be invited back.

Try to recall the areas in which you filled the employer's requirements and the extent to which you were able to convey these aspects of your "ideal candidacy" to the interviewer. These are your *Assets*. On a sheet of paper with this heading, make three columns underneath, headed, respectively:

ASSETS

Job Requirement:_____

_____

My Qualification: _____

_____

Extent Covered in Interview: _____

_____

Points Yet to Be Made:_____

_____

_____

(Repeat for each job requirement.)

On another sheet of paper make three additional columns headed as follows:

LIABILITIES

Job Requirement: _____

_____

My Weakness: _____

_____

Extent Covered in Interview: _____

_____

Points Yet to Be Made: _____

_____

_____

(Repeat for each job requirement.)

Your strategy will consist of internalizing every one of your assets and liabilities, translating the assets into "Ideal Candidate" characteristics for presentation, and the liabilities into potential objections for which you prepare your responses. Prepare a balanced presentation for your interviewer that fairly sets forth both sides of the ledger. Don't try to force-feed the presentation to your interviewer if she prefers to assess your strengths and weaknesses to an agenda of her own. It is more important that you are equipped to deal with all of your assets and liabilities, regardless of sequence, rather than prepare a self-serving speech.

INTERVIEW FOLLOW-UP LETTERS

Your second important job after the interview is to write a letter thanking the interviewer for her time and referring to the two lists (your assets and your liabilities) to decide how to structure the rest of the letter. Here's a follow-up letter from a candidate with a number of qualifications for the position, but who has a possible problem as well:

Gordon F. Cummings

435 Almar Avenue
Pacific Palisades, CA 90616   (213) 454-2616

October 21, 1996

Ms. Terri Crandall
Vice President, Special Products Marketing
KEHM Corporation
1802 Morningside Drive
Allentown, PA 16906

Dear Ms. Crandall:

Thanks very much for your time yesterday regarding the Product Manager's opening at KEHM Corp. As I said before I left your office, this is a job I believe I can do well.

You mentioned four areas in which the successful candidate would need to perform at a consistently high level. They were:

Exposure to asset-based financing - I have managed three products for prospective clients with sizable receivables portfolios. Two of these products were profitable their first year in the marketplace.

Communications skills - In quarterly evaluation reports I consistently rank in the top quartile regarding both verbal communication and listening skills. (I am rated in these areas not only by my supervisor, but my direct reports as well.)

Analytic skills - Before any product proposal is submitted, I routinely conduct exhaustive market research and competitive analysis to assure marketability. The results are further fine-tuned and verified in followup focus groups. In the past four years, seven of the nine products I have submitted were approved, brought to market, and attained profitability.

Ability to inspire and motivate - At Systems International there was zero turnover among employees I hired and trained. Since my departure three department members have themselves been promoted to management positions.

Toward the end of our meeting you expressed a concern about my long-range planning abilities. Both at Convecto and at Systems International I was asked to carve out new product direction on the basis of plans I formulated. (Because the Convecto plan is no longer proprietary, I will gladly share it with you.)

Again, thank you for the courtesy of answering all my questions, and for describing the job and its context so thoroughly. I am very interested in working for KEHM Corp., and would like to repeat my offer to take on a trial assignment that would convince you I am capable of doing the job you want done.

Sincerely,

Gordon F. Cummings

In his letter, the candidate carefully described those of his attributes that matched the job requirements he had identified. He then forcefully addressed and neutralized the objection he had probed during the interview to find. The following three letters reflect slightly different circumstances.

Jack H. Fuller
1010 Mill Stream Dr.
Casper, Wyoming   82333
(307) 647-3807

August 5, 1995

Mr. Peter Salvatore
Three Speed Publishing Company
936 East Wind Drive
Karab, Utah   84741

Dear Mr. Salvatore:

It was a pleasure meeting with you and Joyce Baxter last week to discuss the possibility of joining Three Speed and Merrill. It is clear that many challenges lie ahead as the editorial staff is rebuilt. It's particularly exciting that the company is both old and new -- a strong educational publishing base with the opportunity to pursue new directions.

Three Speed holds a unique position to sell computer education titles in the post-secondary and high school markets. An informal bookstore survey I performed (enclosed) reveals the coverage lists of the major retail publishers (Que, Sybex, Osborne, Microsoft Press). It is important to note the following:

  * None of the titles I surveyed address the reading-level
    requirements of the Three Speed audience; reading level
    appears to vary by author, rather than by publisher policy.

  * Few, if any, provide the requisite activity guides,
    instructors' materials, and companion software demanded by
    the post-secondary and high school markets. Que, with the
    largest line by far, provides only a handful of these
    supplemental pieces for DOS, Introduction to Business Software,
    1-2-3, dBase, and WordPerfect.

It is critical that market intelligence be gathered on the applications and product configurations most in demand in major school districts and post-secondary institutions. The Three-Speed sales force should be involved in this effort as field intelligence will generally be more accurate than third-party reports.

As Joyce suggested, I'm enclosing the expense receipts for my trip to Karab in the amount of $332.

Thank you again for your time. I look forward to speaking with you soon, and wish to reiterate my interest in the editor-in-chief position for electronic publishing. I believe I can bring to this challenging opportunity all the necessary leadership and integrity.

Sincerely yours,

Jack H. Fuller
Enclosures

VIRGENE LENNARTZ
277 WILTON ROAD
NEW CANAAN, CONNECTICUT   06840

January 24, 1994

Dr. Armin Blaufuss
Director of Publications
American Institute of Numerologists
1221 Avenue of the Americas
New York, New York   10036-8775

Dear Dr. Blaufuss:

Thank you for a most enjoyable and informative interview for the position of editor that is open on the Journal of Numerology.

The job description makes me feel comfortable and enthused about the responsibilities and scope of the position. Each requirement draws on those resources that have allowed me to demonstrate my best work during my career.

I believe my qualifications are unique and tailor-made to both fit your needs and help achieve the publication goals you have described. Those qualifications include 15 years in editorial management positions, association and publishing experience, and solid communications-organization-planning ability.

While obtaining my Bachelor of Arts degree in Business Administration, I studied numerology, business finance, and other courses that familiarized me with your field. In addition, my experience in the business world further enhances my ability to relate to the needs and interests of your readers.

In a personal sense, the Journal of Numerology is a publication that I feel good about--a professional journal published by a highly professional organization for a sophisticated and important readership.

I am pleased to be a candidate for the position and appreciate your review and consideration of my credentials.

Very truly yours,

Virgene Lennartz

116

February 5, 1994

Mr. Douglas McClure
Director, Planning and Research
Corrugated Leather Products Corp.
1211 Avenue of the Americas
New York, NY   10036-8775

Dear Mr. McClure:

I enjoyed meeting with you last week.   Although you have received the requested ITT piece, the enclosed extract for Mead Data Central is more representative of my analytical strengths and probably closer to the scale of most Corrugated Leather surveys.

I am looking forward to meeting with you again under less constrained circumstances. I was running late due to train problems, as you may recall.   For this reason I regret that I may have appeared somewhat brusque in my eagerness to learn all could about the research manager position.

My interest in the position remains high, needless to say, because it presents both a challenge and an ideal career move for me.

Sincerely,

Charles Mead

Enclosure

ANTICIPATING OBJECTIONS FOR FOLLOW-UP INTERVIEWS

Unfortunately, you won't fully appreciate our advice about the importance of fact-finding in the first interview until you get a call scheduling your second interview. At that time you will either frantically try to recall the most important problems you'd be asked to solve, or calmly review your notes (some taken during the meeting; some immediately afterward) to line up the points that yet need to be made to see if you and the job are a good match.

Being invited back for a second interview means that you are one of the finalists for the job—or at least one of the semifinalists. Doing your best job from here on requires continued preparation.

Assume you go in to the next interview with both assets and liabilities. If your questioning has been sharp, your listening acute, and your notes complete, you have almost as good a picture of these assets and liabilities as does your interviewer—who will be referring to her own notes. Go through your Assets and Liabilities checklist to help you prepare for the next interview.

If you get the opportunity, make an ally of any company interviewer you meet with whom you might work in some capacity if you get the job. Let her know you're interested in developing a win-win relationship by asking something like:

"What are two or three things you're trying to accomplish that I could assist you with if I came on board?"

Such a question may also yield valuable information about the job itself that you would not have learned otherwise.

REFERENCES

The final test before a job offer is usually a check with your former employers to verify the accuracy of your resume and experiential statements made during the interviews. Be prepared for any closet skeletons to emerge at this time—an additional reminder that any claims you made about your employment or relationships with former employers that stray from truth and accuracy will surely come back to haunt you.

Don't assume that the company's list of references will stop with names you provide. Knowing that you'll try hard to avoid shooting yourself in the foot, they realize that the slate of names you provide won't include anyone who has negative things to say about you. The recruiter Robert Half counsels employers to go out of their way to cultivate references in addition to those provided by the candidate. To let you know what you may be up against, here is his advice to employers on whom to contact, from a self-published booklet called *How to Check References When References Are Hard to Check*. (Remember, this is your prospective boss getting advice on ways to circumvent your reference pool.):

1. *The Obvious.* Those references the candidate gives to you. Ask for many. It can be assumed that those on the bottom of the list are the least important, but may very well be the ones who will be the most candid.

2. *The Immediate Supervisor.* And perhaps the person above the immediate supervisor. These are the people who should know the candidate's work best.

3. *Your counterpart.* It's worth repeating—the person who does the same work you do at the company you're contacting for a reference, is the one most likely to level with you.

4. *Networking.* Ask some of those who give you references to also give you the name of another person to contact in the organization. Then, ask that person to recommend another, and so on. Obviously it's better to not simply talk to a job candidate's "friends."

5. *Personal Reference.* Friends, relatives, teachers, clergy generally have limited value in reference checking, but it certainly can't hurt to contact a few, particularly if there are not enough employer references.

6. *Personnel Department.* This is usually the department least candid in giving references. And, although they can confirm the position and dates of employment, personnel people generally do not have enough day-to-day contact with the employees to rate their on-the-job performance and ability.

7. *Your own contacts.* Your friends, or friends of friends, may know the candidate or someone at the candidate's company. Sometimes, contacts at firms that are competitors of the candidate's firm can give your helpful information particularly if the candidate had high visibility within the industry.

This is what you may be up against. Actually, few employers conduct reference checks as rigorous as those recommended by Half. Nevertheless, some do, and you should assume for safety's sake that all do. Don't hope that an unfortunate incident with a past employer won't surface. Cover yourself by giving your prospective boss a worst-case scenario for those references you think might damage you. If you're working with a recruiter or agency, have a call made in your behalf to get any bad news firsthand.

Letters of reference, by the way, are usually worthless. They're invariably written at termination time, often out of guilt or coercion (or both), filled with superlatives, and never balanced with even the hint of a liability to offset all those assets.

There is an exception. An ex-supervisor asked to put together a letter of reference, for example, will have to organize her thoughts about the former employee's stay at the company to write *anything*. This means that when the reference call comes, she will have done her homework and—if not too long an interval has passed—be able to tick off answers to the caller's questions with a minimum of backing and filling—even using parts of her own letter as a crib sheet.

Here are some topics one recruiter covers in checking the references of candidates in the final stages of the hiring process. Be sure you have gone over the same ground in your own interviews:

- Discuss your personal relationship with the candidate (including length of association).
- How would you assess the candidate's technical competence (strengths and weaknesses) compared to others in similar positions?
- Comment on the candidate's managerial strengths and weaknesses.
- Discuss your impression of the candidate's personal characteristics, including:
  1. Ability to relate to others
  2. Image and presentation
  3. Personal problems that may affect performance on the job (financial, gambling, drinking, etc.)
- What is your knowledge of why the candidate may con-

sider a change at this time (What were the reasons for departure from the previous company?)

- [After informing the reference of the title and parameters of the position for which the candidate is being considered] In your opinion, how will the candidate perform in such a position, and is he the most qualified individual for this position in your circle of contacts?
- What are the candidate's greatest weaknesses?
- Would you rehire this candidate? (Why or why not?)
- Give me a few one- or two-word adjectives that you think best describe the candidate.
- Any additional comments?

You can see that it is possible to cover a lot of subjective ground in such phone conversations. If one reference with a skewed view of your professional or personal characteristics is likely to offer something negative, be sure you have suggested other possible references with a more balanced point of view.

The objection to overcome at this stage of the process will occur if your candidacy is torpedoed by one of your references. You'll know immediately if a relationship that has gone extremely well to this point suddenly sours.

You have nothing to lose by going on the offensive, as for example in the following exchange, just before you thought a job offer was to be made:

INTERVIEWER: Larry, I'm afraid we've decided on someone else for the branch manager's job. I'm sorry.

CANDIDATE: Oh, I'm sorry to hear that. I thought I had all of the qualifications you were looking for. Can you tell me what went wrong?

INTERVIEWER: It's not that anything went "wrong." It's just that we found someone with just a little bit better record than yours.

CANDIDATE: Sorry to press the point, but it may help me in my next situation. The last time we talked, you were going to check a number of my references. Was it something you learned during one of these calls that changed your mind? I can handle it, really. And if there's some deep-seated problem with my candidacy, I should know about it now.

You've gone as far as you can. Your interviewer is under no obligation to tell you the real reason things went sour, but at least you've laid the groundwork for more candor than you've received. If malicious mischief on the part of one of your references turns out to have done you in, at least you'll be able to address it quickly. And if you learn that you have a real problem, you'll be able to address *it* directly.

CHECK OUT THE COMPANY

There are a few things about the company you're thinking of joining that will be useful for you to know before your compensation negotiation interview. Some you may know already from your previous research and reconnaissance work. Other points may not be so obvious. Robert Levering, in *A Great Place to Work*, lists the following company attributes as those meeting his definition. All of them may not be necessary for you to so classify them. Judge for yourself:

- Accepts spontaneous, informal conversation among employees; encourages work-related, informal communication among all levels of employees.
- Has established grievance procedures that employees follow and managers respect; shows a lack of favoritism, bias, or abuse.
- Tolerates individual differences—for example, in a family-like atmosphere it also allows loners to do their jobs without undue pressure.
- Designs jobs so employees can see the results of their work and feel they're making meaningful contributions.
- Integrates all of its policies and practices to treat employees well.
- Shares success with employees through stock ownership plans and profit sharing.
- Produces an employee newsletter that is by and for employees, not controlled and censored by management.

- Maintains such "employee-friendly" policies and practices as paternity leave, flexible scheduling, job-sharing, and tuition reimbursement.[1]

NEGOTIATING COMPENSATION

Talking about compensation doesn't have to be uncomfortable. It is often so because a candidate goes into the negotiation session without preparation and believing he has no power. Both of these disadvantages—one real and one apparent—are correctable.

Preparing to Talk Money

Regardless of how you learned about this job, you should have some idea of what it is worth. Working through a recruiter or employment agency, you need but ask. Because their commission is based on the job's compensation, this information is acquired early in their client deliberations.

If you have worked previously in the industry and function, you will have a good idea of what companies exceed or fall below given salary norms. Often simply asking friends of friends with experience in a field new to you will give you the information you need.

But let's say all of your efforts have failed. You answered a blind ad that sounded good to you, but was skimpy on compensation details. You've found no one who has a good idea of what fair compensation might be for the job. But now, preliminary interviews having all gone well, you find yourself hearing:

"Well, Arthur. I'd like to make you an offer on behalf of CharismaCo." Are you ready?

The key here is flexibility. The rock bottom figure you are willing to accept will be arrived at from sifting through a combination of factors:

- A comparison of your last job duties and compensation with that for the job you are being offered.

---

[1]Robert Levering. *A Great Place to Work* (New York: Random House, 1988.)

- Your financial status (if you have been out of work for several months, you may need a paycheck, period).

Your Negotiating Power

The employer's advantage at this stage of the hiring process is largely illusory. It often results from a feeling on the part of the candidate that the negotiating process is mostly about groveling for dollars, and therefore unseemly. This leads to a psychological vulnerability that works nicely to the employer's advantage.

All of your notes from previous interviews will tell you how good a match you are for the position. The job offer alone tells you you're the best person the company has seen. Beyond that, knowing what problems you can solve, both immediately and long range, should be on the tip of your tongue for leverage when you and the employer begin to talk specific dollars. Go back to the specific job requirements and your respective job strengths to refresh your memory.

The Negotiating Process

If you have little or no information regarding the job's compensation, the interviewer has an immediate advantage. She'll probably ask you about your most recent compensation package, both to open the topic and to find out what she's up against. Answer honestly and concisely, including in your figure the amount of all bonuses and benefits.

At this point you might hear something like: "What kind of money were you expecting to make?" Your response at this point could be: "Well, my package at Solarlux was $51,000. From the way you describe this job, I'd say it would be worth about $56,000." You're asking for a 10 percent boost, which is not unreasonable.

You might also try to turn the edge by answering with a question of your own, such as: "That's a good question. Could you tell me the salary range for this position? Then I'd have a better idea of where I might fit into it." This reasonable request is acceded to in most situations.

If the job represents an upgrading of responsibilities for you, your response would be a figure near the bottom of the range. Never suggest a figure much beyond the range midpoint. Above that will be allowance for growth in the job, and the raises that would reward that growth. To get beyond the top of the range you would need a promotion, unless the company were to restructure compensation for either the position or the department.

The Employment Contract

Those of you approaching the six-figure salary level—or many of you in the sales field—may suggest that your final compensation be formalized in a written contract or letter of agreement. Such a document will include some or all of the following provisions:

1. Term or duration of employment
2. Description of duties
3. Base salary
4. Performance bonuses of various kinds
5. Medical, dental, and life insurance
6. Retirement benefits
7. Relocation expenses where applicable (sometimes to include company purchase and disposition of the old residence, and/or company assumption of closing costs of the new residence)
8. Low, or no-interest loans
9. Periodic payment of company-related expenses of various kinds
10. "Luxury perks," such as limousines and club memberships
11. Contingency clauses (often called golden parachutes) in the event of company change of ownership
12. Severance conditions (amount, frequency, and duration)
13. Contract termination conditions (for both employee and employer)

See John Tarrant's *Perks and Parachutes,* listed at the end of this chapter, for a thorough discussion of employment contracts and contract negotiation.

Regardless of whether you utilize the employment contract, check through the list above to determine which items may have relevance for your deliberations.

The key is to stay flexible in your negotiations and not think in terms of a base salary that may not be changeable. The following exchange, from the *JOB-BRIDGE* career transition program, shows how a candidate recovering from a job loss was still able to leverage his qualifications into an offer both employer and employee were happy with.

INTERVIEWER: Well, it's been a long process, Gordon, but we'd like to offer you the marketing manager's job.

CANDIDATE: I'm delighted.

INTERVIEWER: What would you say to a base of $61,000?

CANDIDATE: Actually, I'm a bit disappointed.

INTERVIEWER: We're talking about a performance bonus that should run another $8,000, if things go the way we hope they will. I should have mentioned that at the outset.

CANDIDATE: Still, that's only a five percent increase over my Systems International salary. A little less, actually.

INTERVIEWER: Well, what did you have in mind?

CANDIDATE: I was really expecting $70,000—plus the bonus.

INTERVIEWER: I'm afraid that's out of the question. There has to be some growth built into the range for a possible raise at review time.

CANDIDATE: Well, maybe there's some give in that area. Is it possible for the review to be moved back to three months?

INTERVIEWER: We're pretty locked in there, I'm afraid. Company policy is a six-month review after hire, and annually thereafter. No exceptions. You know, considering the fact that you don't have a paycheck at all right now, I think this is quite a generous offer.

CANDIDATE: Terry, I don't think that's a factor. I have a lot to offer you, irrespective of why I am available for this position right now. I'm still very interested, and I think my management skills, telemarketing accomplishments, and investment banking exposure all make me the ideal candidate for the job.

INTERVIEWER: Well, we're obviously very interested in you or I wouldn't have made an offer in the first place.

CANDIDATE: Well, how about this? If I were to receive a sign-on bonus, it wouldn't interrupt your salary structure for this level and it could go some distance toward making up the differential.

INTERVIEWER: What did you have in mind?

CANDIDATE: $7,500?

INTERVIEWER: (Pause.) I think I could get you $4,000.

CANDIDATE: You've got a deal.

INTERVIEWER: That's great.

Critique The candidate:
1. Remained flexible, and looked for alternatives other than a frozen base salary that would improve his position (if a sign-on bonus isn't practical in your situation, try to negotiate an earlier raise or promotion date).
2. Handled the reference to his out-of-work status without being defensive and with positive effect.
3. Restated his major accomplishments.
4. Demonstrated how his goals would benefit the employer as well as himself.

Unless there is absolutely no doubt in your mind about a job offer, sleep on it. You may think of something after you leave the interview that will affect your decision. Say something like:

"Thank you very much for the offer. I'd like to give it serious consideration and get back to you on Friday. Is that all right with you?"

or,

"Will you be putting that in writing?"

If you're fortunate enough to have two job offers to choose from, make another "Column A" and "Column B" list, comparing the respective benefits of one offer to another: by job, boss, company, corporate culture, opportunity for advancement, opportunities for training, community, compensation, perks and benefits—and make your decision accordingly.

ADDITIONAL READING

Bird, Caroline. *Everything a Woman Needs to Get Paid What She's Worth.* New York: David McKay Company, Inc., 1973. Describes tactics hundreds of women have used in overcoming objections to earning money commensurate with their abilities.

Fisher, Roger. *Getting to Yes: Negotiating Agreements Without Giving In.* Boston: Houghton Mifflin Company, 1985. How to separate the people from the problem and work together to create options that satisfy both parties.

Tarrant, John. *Perks and Parachutes.* New York: Simon & Schuster, 1985. Bargaining-table psychology and strategy; common pitfalls in employment contracts and how to avoid them. Examples of actual *Fortune* 500 company contracts.

7

Flourishing On Your New Job

It may have taken you longer than you thought it would, but here you are. We hope your new job is an exciting one, and that you accepted it for all of the right reasons. The important thing is to think of this new assignment not as an end, but as a beginning.

One of the lessons that may have helped get you this far is an improved ability to communicate. It is this skill that will be your best ally in the weeks and months ahead. No matter what your function or industry, it is crucial to keep all lines of communication open: to your customers (both inside and outside the organization), to your boss, to your direct reports, to your colleagues.

This means listening to these constituencies as carefully as you did to the interviewer when she first described your new job. It means asking the questions that will neutralize any new objections before they become brush fires. It means transmitting information distinctly and unambiguously—both orally and on paper.

The bottom line, after all, is that unless you have a written contract with your employer, you are one of the vast majority of those employees serving "at will." (You have probably guessed it already—at the *employer's* will.) If you don't satisfactorily perform your job, in other words, there will come a time when you are asked to leave it. This is indeed the flip side of "flourishing on the job," but it is also important to keep in mind that your employer is in business to make money, not to keep you happy. If you help make the company money you keep management happy—as a result you will be happy, and remain employed. This is *your* end of the implied bargain.

MAINTAINING BRIDGES

Before we get into some of the particulars of flourishing on your new job, there is one remaining task that will help to maintain your professional continuum. Your network is now considerably more extensive than it was before you began your search. You need to inform everyone who has been of assistance to you that, with their help, you have accomplished your goal.

For friends and colleagues nearby who have given you a hand, a phone call will suffice. For others, including helpful executive recruiters (who may have the opportunity to be helpful again), write a note with a few details regarding your new assignment. On the facing page is a sample you can adapt for your own purposes.

KEYS TO JOB LONGEVITY

To allow your job to develop into long-term employment, there are two more things you must do: 1) Master the job, and 2) become a fully functioning member of your work group.

Mastering the Job

Your readiness to perform any part of your new job is composed of your ability and your motivation—your skill and your will, so to speak.

RORY CAMPBELL

4610 Allentown Road
Weehauken, NJ 07492

June 28, 1995

Mr. R. Frank Wolfson
Teriyaki Recruitment Emporium
1757 Black Rock Turnpike
Morristown, NJ 07960

Dear Frank:

This letter is to let you know that I have completed my
search, and to say thanks for your interest and encouragement
over the past several months.

I have accepted an offer to join Wranaco, Inc., as Senior Vice
President of Marketing. I will be located in White Plains,
and also in Manhattan at 70 Park Avenue. My responsibilities
include corporate brands, with major concentration on the
metal ore businesses. Wranco is a Fortune 500 company with
additional manufacturing interests in intimate apparel brands
such as Speedo, White Stag, and Milady's Excellent Adventure.

I have appreciated your help during this period and trust you
will call on me whenever I can reciprocate.

Best personal regards,

/mb

Some new hires are very skilled, thanks to their previous experience, training, or education. Others come on board as trainees, solely because of their potential, and are usually highly motivated.

Regardless of your level of technical skills, you need to develop a precise understanding of what the job calls for—which includes a combination of your supervisor's expectations, together with any expressed or implied corporate mission. The communication skills mentioned above will be instrumental in internalizing these two elements.

Your motivation, on the other hand, is a mix of security, confidence, incentive, and drive; in varying proportions. Its level often depends on how close you are to mastering your job. It takes some new employees longer than others for confidence to match drive. When the skill package doesn't fall into place as quickly as originally hoped, in fact, confidence sometimes flags. If this happens to you, be patient. Always be willing to take on additional responsibilities, but don't overextend yourself. (On the other hand, the high performing sales rep who hates paperwork probably will *never* find that part of his job motivating.)

Joining the Team

Outplacement counselors report that after displacement by downsizing, their corporate clients attribute the highest cause of termination to "poor chemistry." As it turns out, this hazy term is a catchall for a number of causes of discharge discussed in considerable detail in Chapter 1 of our first book, *Conquer Resume Objections*. It is also a euphemism for several more egregious factors sometimes at work when people simply don't get along—among them fear, envy, jealousy, arrogance, and disrespect.

Teams are complex entities. The success of each is dependent on a fragile interplay among the members based on real and perceived hierarchies, ego involvement, skill interaction, and communication abilities.

Incorporating a new member into a team can change the group's composition completely. The smaller the group, the greater this possibility.

Even if you are filling a defined void in the group, you do not automatically become accepted as a member. Everyone else has to rediscover how to work together. It is now a new group. Everyone, including you—even if you are the new group leader—will have to adapt to make the new group successful. Your ultimate goal, of course, is a level of commitment and shared accountability that will allow you to fulfill the team's objectives successfully.

TRACKING YOUR PERFORMANCE

Keilty, Goldsmith & Company, a California management consulting firm, has designed a checklist (shown below) for use with its corporate clients that analyzes and prescribes improvement for employee performance. Part of this checklist is reprinted in adapted form here. Use it as a true/false indicator to plot your interactive progress with those groups applicable to your situation.

Ask these questions of yourself at three-month intervals to be sure you are on the right track. To make the responses even more useful, create a "One to five" scale for each question, rather than using true/false responses. (One could be "always" and Five "never," with appropriate gradations in between.)

Ask a colleague to second guess your answers to provide an objective reality check. Work on the two or three items that are causing you the most trouble during any three-month period. (Select no more than three items for concentration. More will cause you to lose focus in evaluating your effectiveness.) Keeping on top of your responsibilities in this fashion will add to your value as an employee—as well as provide complete notes in preparation for any formal performance review your company requires.

WITH YOUR CUSTOMERS

- Consistently treat my customers as a top priority?
- Am more committed to customer satisfaction than in meeting short-term goals?

- Clearly communicate the importance of customers to those with whom I work?
- Discourage destructive comments about my customers?
- Encourage input from my customers?
- Listen to input from customers rather than assume knowledge of their needs?
- Act to solve customer problems in a timely manner?
- Search for better ways to help customers?
- Make honest, realistic commitments to customers?
- Live up to commitments made to customers?

WITH MANAGEMENT

- Inspire pride in my new organization?
- Personally support higher management's decisions?
- Believe in the values of the organization?
- Discourage destructive comments about the organization or its management?
- Communicate improvements that would benefit my organization?
- Generate useful approaches to improve the way we do things?
- Strive to get the most out of organization resources available to me?
- Strive to increase the organization's return on assets?

WITH DIRECT REPORTS AND COLLEAGUES

- Consistently show respect and concern for people as individuals?
- Inspire pride in our work team?

- Help people feel like "winners?"
- Recognize top performance?
- Listen to others' ideas?
- Set challenging standards for co-workers?
- Give constructive performance feedback in a timely manner?
- Strive to improve co-workers' performance from acceptable to excellent?
- Recognize and reinforce improvements in performance?
- Deal effectively with performance problems?

IN YOUR IMMEDIATE ASSIGNMENT

- Committed to excellence in task achievement?
- Take action to get things done?
- Focus others' efforts on achieving what is most important?
- Inspire pride in our work?
- Communicate the belief that excellence will be achieved?
- Try innovative strategies, rather than "play it safe?"
- Act on ideas and suggestions from others in a timely manner?
- Emphasize finding solutions rather than "placing blame?"
- Willing to take risks in trying out new ideas?

AGAINST YOUR PERSONAL POTENTIAL

- Practice integrity in dealing with others?
- Take responsibility and ownership for my decisions?
- Lead by example?

- Am confident of my actions and decisions?

- Am honest and ethical in my business transactions?

- Encourage constructive criticism?

- Work to improve my job-related performance?

- Willing to admit my mistakes?

- Avoid ego-dominated actions?

- Act on constructive advice in a timely manner?

GROWING IN THE JOB

Improve your visibility in the company by volunteering to serve on inter-divisional committees as openings become available. Let your boss know that you'd like to increase your exposure in order to get a better idea of the total corporate picture. (P.S. You'll also be in a better position to hear about vacancies of interest to you in other sectors of the company as they occur, as well as become better known to executives doing the hiring.)

Offer to speak or prepare reports for industry or functional organizations and trade shows. Don't be discouraged by your first attempts. They won't be representative of your performance level after you gain additional experience and confidence. If you are reluctant to pursue such a course, consider taking a public speaking class to improve your skill and confidence level in this area.

If you are promoted to a managerial level from a staff position, leave nothing to chance regarding your transition. If your company does not have an orientation program for new managers, ask for tips from your boss and read any self-help materials that will help you solve any new problems that might emerge due to your new responsibilities. Barron's Educational Series, for example, has published a paperback series of "Business Success" titles, offering assistance in running meetings, conducting interviews, making presentations, motivating people, and other skill sets critical to the new manager's success. See the end-of-chapter bibliography for a complete list of titles.

NEGOTIATING A RAISE

It is natural for you to want to be recognized for your effectiveness when you handle your job well—financially, as well as in other ways. When you are able to get the most out of yourself, you enjoy your work more—an anticipated consequence is that you will also make more money.

How you ask for a raise is important. But how you prepare for the request is usually even more important. The more valuable a member of your team and the company you are, the stronger your case will be for getting a raise.

Even so, most workers find it difficult to confront their boss and ask the question. Many employees in large companies don't even bother, feeling that the salary negotiation process is completely beyond their control. Workers in smaller companies find it no less difficult.

The biggest reason for this reluctance is fear of rejection. Even if the boss is totally satisfied with your work, but cites other factors as mitigating against the raise, it still is a rejection. Most of us hope we'll get the increase *without* asking, in which case risking rejection will not be an issue.

John Tarrant, in *How to Negotiate a Raise*, suggests two lines of strategy in preparing for a raise request[1], broken down as follows:

1. Gauge the "official" position of the boss and the organization, by examining . . .

   - The pattern of raises given to you and others in similar jobs

---

[1]John Tarrant, *How to Negotiate a Raise*. New York: Van Nostrand Reinhold Co., 1976.

- The extent to which compensation is part of a fixed budget process

- The degree of freedom your boss has in deciding on raises

- The current condition of business within the company and the industry

- The company's plans for the immediate future.

2. Study your boss's personal position by reviewing . . .

- Her overall pattern of conduct with regard to you

- The degree to which she praises or criticizes specific parts of your performance

- Her own position in the firm and her ambitions for growth

- The extent to which she takes you for granted

- Her knowledge of just what you do and how valuable you are.

By carefully reviewing both the boss's official and personal perspectives, you should be able to reach certain conclusions about your prospects for a raise, and the best way to get one. If your case is particularly strong, of course, your chances improve. And if you time your request to coincide with an especially good piece of news regarding company, department, or (your) personal performance, your chances improve exponentially.

Taking a hard line—an explicit or implicit threat to resign, for example—is an option when other strategies have failed. Even then, though, it is wise to keep in mind the following possible caveats to your approach:

- How strongly does the boss feel about keeping me on?

- Is she likely to hold a grudge against me?

- Is getting the raise worth the possible bitter aftertaste?

Even if your answers to these questions clear the way for such an extreme decision as threatening resignation, it is folly to follow through on your threat without another job to go to. The exception? Your strong feeling that not having a job is preferable to keeping your current job without the raise you seek.

KEEPING A PAPER TRAIL

Finally, record an extra copy of every memo, letter, report, and proposal you write that contributes to the company or department's success, or to your personal growth. This record can be used in your periodic performance reviews to give you ready documentation for promotions or raises that may need reinforcing. They are also valuable raw data in updating your resume, and can serve (as they lose their proprietary status) as corroboration for accomplishments that may be useful in interviewing for your next job.

Also, be sure you are armed in case you need to defend your tenure on the job at some future date. Your employer is keeping a file on you, to be sure. And "the one with the biggest stack of papers wins," goes the labor lawyers' saw about employee-employer lawsuits. At a minimum, make sure you save a copy of the following:

- Job application form
- Aptitude tests and any other pre-employment evaluations (if you can get them)
- Company employee handbook
- All memos and letters (whether laudatory or critical)
- Written warnings or notices of disciplinary action
- Significant memos, letters and reports authored by you.

This is not paranoia, but sound survival practice. Keep this file at home, not in the office. Your personal records may not always be secure at work and could be viewed inadvertently by someone looking for work-related material in your absence.

IF YOU'RE "IRREPLACEABLE"

There are a couple of danger signs that should alert you to the possibility of trouble in your job. The first has to do with those of you who are managers and have an illusion that you are "irreplaceable."

Everett Suters, author of *Succeed in Spite of Yourself*, says that irreplaceable managers block the advancement of their subordinates; they're a nuisance to superiors who end up having to handle problems for them in their absence; and because of the undue stress they place on themselves, they're a threat to their department's performance—and possibly to the health of department members as well.[2]

Here are a few ways to tell if this career roadblock might be in your way. If you can plead guilty to more than half of them, you need to think about a change:

You

[ ] You're a reluctant delegator, and give so much direction that you siphon off your subordinates' decision-making authority

[ ] You're usually too busy to discuss matters with your people, except before or after the business day

[ ] You always have more work than your subordinates

[ ] You either don't take vacations or take off just one day at a time

[ ] You call in constantly while you're away, trying to do your job long distance

---

[2]Everett Suters, *Succeed in Spite of Yourself*. New York: Van Nostrand Reinhold Co., 1973.

[ ]   In your absence, your boss often has to step in to put out fires

Your Staff

[ ]   Your employees' skills are essentially unchanged from a year ago

[ ]   Above-average turnover in your department

[ ]   No one on your staff is promotable

[ ]   None of your employees are able to fill in while you're away

[ ]   Your employees rarely come to you with new ideas or new ways of doing their jobs

[ ]   Your staff members rarely make decisions or solve problems without your input

Can your organization do without you? If your inclination is to say no, you need to rethink your managerial priorities. This may simply be a matter of inability to spread the work around and trust staff members. On the other hand, there may be a psychological need for you to be so firmly in charge.

If you aren't able to take the following corrective action without emotional trauma, the situation may be beyond you and call for professional assistance:

- Start slowly. Don't leave for a three-week holiday after giving your staff six weeks of work.

- Give your staff one or two projects while you're still around to provide direction and support.

- Define your expectations by establishing a series of checkpoints; then trust your employees with the details.

- On your next trip for two days or more, don't call in. Instead, make written arrangements to ensure that all bases are covered by specifically designated members of your department.

Delegating properly will teach your employees skills they need to advance their careers. The added benefit is that when a promotion possibility becomes available, you will be able to name your successor and assure corporate continuity.

WHEN TO GO OVER YOUR BOSS'S HEAD

A solution to workplace injustice that often occurs to those who feel unfairly treated by their bosses is to seek a hearing one step up. The problem with going over your boss's head to complain is that blowing off a little steam may be the extent of your accomplishment. An even greater downside: the possible repercussions when your boss finds out.

There are steps you can take, though, to minimize the risks and increase chances of getting a fair hearing. Here is advice from Peter Wylie and Mardy Grothe, authors of the book *Problem Bosses: Who They Are and How to Deal With Them:*[3]

> *Pick the right boss.* Your boss's boss may indeed be the one to consult. You may decide otherwise, however, if that person hired your boss, or if the two are diehard allies.
>
> To find the manager most likely to give you the best hearing, make a list of the best candidates, and ask yourself these questions:
>
> - *How fair is this person?* If you have reason to believe the boss you're considering is an unfair judge, think again.
>
> - *Is this person a good problem solver?* You can take your troubles to the most understanding executive in the world, but if you're talking to a fence sitter, you're wasting your time.

[3]©1986 by Mardy Grothe and Peter Wylie, Facts on File Publications.

- *How influential is this person?* Don't confuse rank with clout. Sometimes an executive lower in the pecking order can have more pull because of additional unofficial power.

Preparing Your Presentation. Once you've picked your person, prepare what you want to say and how you'll say it. Here are a few suggestions:

- *State your purpose.* Define your mission up front, explaining why you've asked to see this person and what you want to discuss. This stage setting is particularly important when the manager you've approached knows nothing about the situation.

- *Be brief and to the point.* If you have good documentation you won't need to say a lot to make your case.

- *Talk candidly.* Two areas worth covering: how your boss makes you feel (angry, resentful, humiliated), and the detrimental effects she has on your work performance.

- *Offer a solution.* Your meeting will be more productive if you come prepared with several suggestions on how this person can help you resolve the situation.

A PARTING SHOT

We're pleased to have been able to take you to this stage of your career and hope our advice has been useful in getting you from point A to point B (or, for some of you, perhaps from point Q to point R).

If you've gotten as far as this page, we assume that you've found some answers in one or more of the following areas:

1. Reconnaissance strategy on targeted companies

2. Making the best interview first impression

3. Becoming the ideal candidate

4. Testing for predictable interview objections

5. Overcoming camouflaged objections

6. Making the close; negotiating the best compensation

7. Flourishing on your new job

If you need assistance in the following areas, you'll find them in *Conquer Resume Objections*:

1. Defining your specific career problems

2. Pinpointing your career direction

3. Organizing your job search

4. Developing a marketing plan

5. Writing your master resume and cover letter

6. Overcoming resume objections

If there are aspects of your particular interest areas that have not been covered to your satisfaction, please write to tell us, so we can address them in the next edition. If you have suggestions for other topics that you would like to see covered, we want to know.

ADDITIONAL READING

Barron's Success Business Guides. Hauppauge, NY: Barron's Educational Series, Inc., 1991. Eight paperbacks covering crucial aspects of the responsibilities to help the new manager to a successful transition. Titles include: *Conducting Better Job Interviews, How to Negotiate a Bigger Raise, Make Presentations With Confidence, Motivating People, Running a Meeting That Works, Using the Telephone More Effectively, Winning With Difficult People, Writing Effective Letters and Memos.*

Catalyst. *Making the Most of Your First Job.* New York: Putnam, 1981. Primarily for women: How to survive a first job, personally and professionally; finding a niche at work; getting noticed; learning on the job; coping with stress; communicating well.

Covey, Stephen R. *The Seven Habits of Highly Effective People.* New York: Simon & Schuster, 1989. Twenty-five years of research have produced a way for readers to integrate the workways of an extremely successful minority. Includes exercises.

Career Without Limits. New York: John Wiley & Sons, 1989. Hands-on techniques for preparing for opportunity—even making it come to you. Case studies from a wide variety of industries.

Gabarro, John J. and John P. Kotter, "Managing Your Boss," *Harvard Business Review*, May–June, 1993, pp. 150–157. Forming compatible relationships with your superior is essential to being effective on the job. Demonstrates ways to build mutual respect and understanding.

Josefowitz, Natasha & Herman. *Fitting In: How to Get a Good Start in Your New Job.* Reading, MA: Addison-Wesley, 1988. Numerous cases dealing with issues confronting employees in new jobs.

A

Thinker, Visionary, Driver, Friend: Four Interviewer Personalities

Here's our premise: The first few minutes with an interviewer representing each of the four personality types described on pages 26–32 can lead to significantly different job interviews, even when covering the same subject matter.

Knowing that different kinds of scenarios can develop in an interview, depending on who sits on the other side of the desk—and being able to adjust accordingly—should be enough to cause subtle differences in your interview style.

At the other extreme, such an awareness can keep you from offending an interviewer with your job in her hands. After all, the point here is not to put something over on anyone, but to know your customer to the extent that your responses and questions keep attention on content and away from a style that may jar or irritate. We'll show you what we mean, by playing out an interview-opening scenario for a specific job opening—with each of the four interviewer types listed above:

A candidate is up for a corporate communications position with the following specifications:

1. To coordinate the development of a corporate image program and organize a corporate advertising campaign.
2. To act as a consultant to the company's product managers regarding the development and placement of all product advertising and divisional press relations.
3. To work with members of the Executive Committee regarding their public appearances, assisting them with speeches, approving news releases, and initiating all press contact.

The candidate prepared for this interview by conducting the research as discussed in Chapter 2 of *Conquer Resume Objections*, and the reconnaissance interviews discussed in Chapter 1 of *Conquer Interview Objections*. In addition to this he prepared:

- An all-purpose introduction or one-minute autobiography, that he could use in its entirety or draw from as needed.
- A summary of the job requirements (as listed above), to enable him to test his understanding of what was needed against his position-related strengths.

Thus armed, he had the best possible chance of learning all he could about the job and resolving any objections that might arise during his interviews. But there are subtle differences in the way he got his points across in each instance, all dictated by the style of the person on the other side of the desk. Hypothetical cases such as these are usually overdrawn to some extent, just so the point can be made clearly. For this reason, it's important for you to look at the scenarios below as hypothetical and potentially useful to you to the degree that you make them so. Let's start with the candidate's one-minute commercial:

> While working on my M.B.A. at St. John's, I wrote and sold newspaper ads, which is how I got my start in the business. My first job after receiving the M.B.A. was with Brendon & Brendon, the number one agency in Columbus. After working as Terry Brendon's assistant for three years— as good a grounding in all aspects of the agency business as I could have hoped for—I decided to move to New York, where I got a job with McCall Peterson (on the strength of a good reference from Mr. Brendon). My specialty was working with private companies that intended to go public.

My job was to help them get their message across to the equity markets, as well as their customers, suppliers, employees, and local communities, to make sure their initial public offerings were as successful as possible.

Ten years ago one of my clients, Washington Wood, hired me to head its public relations department, and since that time the company has grown ten-fold. My responsibilities include corporate image advertising, corporate press and public relations, and coordinating all divisional advertising.

For each of the three job requirements the candidate wrote up three accomplishments from previous jobs that matched these requirements. Following these he listed all of his skills that similarly demonstrated an ability to do the job. From his point of view he was ready . . . but his four interviewers will be the judge of that:

THINKER

The interviewer's office is neat, with two large bookcases on one wall, and a work table set at a right angle to her desk. Atop it is a computer, which is on.

INTERVIEWER: Come in. Sit down.(*points to a chair next to a large mahogany table, empty except for neat stack of computer printouts*). Thanks for coming in. If you don't mind, I'd like to get right to the point here. Can you tell me first why you think you are qualified for this job?

CANDIDATE: As I understand it, the successful candidate will have three major assignments:

1. Coordinating the development of a corporate image program and organizing a corporate advertising campaign;

2. Acting as a consultant to the company's product managers regarding the development and placement of all product advertising and divisional press relations; and

3. Working with members of the Executive Committee regarding public appearances, assisting them with

speeches, working on news releases, and initiating all press contact.

Does this capture it accurately?

INTERVIEWER: So far, so good. By the way, what do *you* mean by corporate image?

CANDIDATE: Successful organizations have a vision of who they are or who they want to be. It is not just a case of adding together what all the divisions do.

Before any campaign is launched, there must be a consensus on the corporate mission to develop an image that effectively communicates that mission—or image—to all intended audiences.

With that mission in mind, it is possible to develop strategies, along with a long-range plan for each of the product divisions.

INTERVIEWER: Can you support that?

CANDIDATE: Well, think of the former Maytag campaign. What image comes to mind? The serviceman who never gets a call. They didn't say they had the best repair service in the industry. They said that so much quality was built into the machine that it never *needed* a repair.

INTERVIEWER: Good point. Now, can you apply it to this job?

CANDIDATE: It's the same image across all the divisions, but each management team had to develop and implement a different set of steps to build into its products that same level of quality.

INTERVIEWER: OK. So much for theoretical abstraction. Tell me now how that makes you the best person for this job.

CANDIDATE: Well. First of all, I need to know if my assessment of your requirements was correct.

INTERVIEWER: Let's say that it was. How would you fit in?

CANDIDATE: I need to ask one more question first.

INTERVIEWER: Go ahead.

CANDIDATE: Is my definition of "corporate image" consistent with yours?

INTERVIEWER: Yes. Continue.

CANDIDATE: OK, then, back to your three requirements:
1. Development of the corporate image, which we've defined;
2. Act as consultant to the division product managers, which we've alluded to; and
3. Work with the Executive Committee in a number of areas.

I'd like to give you a couple of examples of ways I have demonstrated my competence in each of these three areas. First of all . . . .

Critique

All of the candidate's questions and responses were consistent with the Thinker's personality and priorities:
1. The candidate first tested his knowledge of the job's requirements before volunteering any particulars about his ability to perform it (as advocated in Chapter 3).
2. He lost neither his cool nor his train of thought when the interviewer asked him to give her his definition of "corporate image" and called upon his research to give a satisfactory response.
3. When asked a second time to give his credentials, he made sure his job assessment was accurate before answering. Even then, he first asked the interviewer to verify the accuracy of the previously offered definition.

VISIONARY

The interviewer comes from behind a large, wooden desk to greet the candidate. A number of stacks of folders cover both the desk and a nearby credenza.

INTERVIEWER: Good morning. (*Shakes hands with candidate.*) Would you like a cup of coffee?
CANDIDATE: Yes, thank you.
INTERVIEWER: Milk? Sugar?

CANDIDATE: A little of each, thank you.

INTERVIEWER: (*To assistant:*) Two regulars, please. (*To candidate:*) I hope you had no difficulty finding us.

CANDIDATE: Not at all. Your directions were perfect. I grew up here in the city, so it all fell into place very quickly.

INTERVIEWER: So what do you know about us?

CANDIDATE: That you've been around for twenty-odd years. That your growth curve in the past four years has been enviable. That you're privately held with an idea to possibly change that in the near future, and that might be one reason I'm here.

INTERVIEWER: You're pretty close. To fill in the blanks, we're going to be going in a direction we haven't traveled before and we don't want to be making it up as we go along. That's where you *could* come in.

According to your resume, you've gone through this drill before. Can you walk me through that part of your background?

CANDIDATE: Sure. For six years at McCall Peterson, all I did was help client companies go public. I've written speeches for company officers (here are a couple, by the way, if you'd like to read them later); handled corporate image problems; and generally coached top executives in handling their dealings with the media and the public.

INTERVIEWER: Did this get to be formula work, or were there a lot of crazy problems you had to deal with from company to company?

CANDIDATE: There weren't any two that were alike. Again, I have two plans here that represent the opposite ends of the spectrum. They're not proprietary, so I can leave them with you for a while.

INTERVIEWER: I appreciate that. They should be helpful in seeing how you dealt with long-term implications.

CANDIDATE: Is that going to be the toughest part of this, do you think?

INTERVIEWER: Well, yes. For example, what happens down the road when we present ourselves to the equity markets? Nobody here has ever spoken to—and certainly never addressed—a group of Wall Street analysts.

CANDIDATE: Well obviously you've been analyzing the challenge in terms of the audiences to be addressed. Your strategy is correct, so far as I can tell. Each audience requires different tactics, and, as you indicated, with some you are further along than with others.

One client I helped with an initial public offering was in many respects a company like yours: a family-owned equipment manufacturer, three product lines, and sales in the same neighborhood as yours. Would it be helpful if I told you about how we structured their IPO?

INTERVIEWER: Please go ahead.

Critique

1.   The candidate demonstrated solid research by his awareness of the company's background and future intent.

2.   In "walking the interviewer through his background," he mentioned only experience that related directly to the open position in order to make her comfortable with his ability to do the job.

3.   The interviewer's priorities, in addition to various outward manifestations of her personality, indicated the creative approach of a Visionary. The candidate effectively addressed her interest in long-range concerns and innovation.

4.   With this level of understanding, the candidate felt comfortable enough with the interviewer to volunteer statements he knew would strike a resonant chord and advance his cause.

DRIVER

The interviewer's office is conventionally laid out, with undistinguished prints on the walls. Neat stacks of papers line most flat surfaces.

INTERVIEWER: Come on in and sit down. (Motions candidate to chair piled with papers. Walks quickly to chair and moves papers to his desk, to give candidate a place to sit.

CANDIDATE: Thank you.

INTERVIEWER: You're here for the corporate advertising job, right?

CANDIDATE: Yes, sir.

INTERVIEWER: You think you can handle it?

CANDIDATE: If my understanding of the requirements is accurate, I'm sure I can.

INTERVIEWER: OK, let's go through them. Tell me what you've done helping other private companies to go public.

CANDIDATE: That was the only job I had for six years. We took eight clients public during that time, and I got the message out to the various audiences—equity markets, customers, suppliers, employees, community leaders—and they coached the company officers on the most effective ways of dealing with the media and the public.

INTERVIEWER: What was the bottom line? How do you know it worked?

CANDIDATE: My clients thought so. I have eight phone numbers here for the CEOs of each of them. Which ones would you like to call . . . ?

Critique

1. The candidate began to work with the Driver's brusque, forceful style immediately. When asked if he could handle the job, his answer indicated a healthy self-confidence in his abilities ("If my understanding of the requirements is accurate, I'm sure I can.")

2. His answer to the first detailed job-related question was complete and specific, and delivered crisply.

3. His challenge to the interviewer to check with his clients to verify the quality of his work was a calculated risk. Actually, nothing less likely would have satisfied the interviewer, the way her question was worded ("How do you know it worked?") left little room for any response short of pulling testimonials out of his briefcase, written by these same clients. This tactic was an excellent choice for the Driver, but probably would be less successful with any of the other three kinds of interviewers.

FRIEND

Memorabilia fills empty spaces all over the office, including the pictures on the wall. The furniture could have been delivered directly from her den.

INTERVIEWER: Hello. May I get you some coffee?(Shakes candidate's hand, nearly knocking a stack of papers from a cluttered desk as she does so.)

CANDIDATE: Yes, thanks. I'd be happy to join you.

INTERVIEWER: Let's get some together. The pantry is just down the hall. That way you can fix it the way you like it.

CANDIDATE: (Looking at pictures on bookcase as they leave the office.) I see baseball is still popular around here. Is that a Little League team?

INTERVIEWER: My son's team. My husband is the manager.

CANDIDATE: Great. How'd you do this year?

INTERVIEWER: Not great, but we had a lot of fun.

CANDIDATE: Is Oswego still the powerhouse it was when I played around here?

INTERVIEWER: Oh, that's right; you did grow up around here. No, the team to beat these days is North Aurora—has been for the past three or four years.

CANDIDATE: Well, I'd like to have been around to see that. North Aurora was the dregs back when I played. We couldn't stand them.

INTERVIEWER: Well, this is today, as they say. Can I interest you in talking about the job we've got to sell here?

CANDIDATE: You bet. I've been thinking a lot about it over the past few days . . . .

Critique

Don't rush the Friend. Bide your time and be ready to come out swinging—when she says the time is right.

B

It Worked For Them

All job seekers have individual situations that set them apart from others and affect the way they conduct their job search. But it is not just their *situations* that set these people apart. It is also the way they respond to the circumstances in which they find themselves. The following case studies tell the stories of people like yourself, who overcame objections of one kind or another to get the jobs they wanted—although in some instances they weren't aware that the path they took was open to them at the time. See if you can find in their stories suggestions for ways out of your predicament. Look also for the reasons for which each might have made the various decisions that led to success. In those instances where resumes or cover letters were part of the strategy, they are included.

PROFILE: "Sidney Hawkes," 62, was senior buyer for a major corporation until recently. On the Monday morning he returned with his wife from a one-week Caribbean vacation, he was asked to report to his boss's office. There he was informed that "early retirement" would begin at the end of that business day.

Sidney's shock at losing his job was profound—to the extent that for the next two weeks he hid this information from his wife, thinking it would adversely affect her heart condition. Every morning he left "for work" as usual, coming home at his regular time each evening.

Sidney was offered minimal outplacement from his employer, which consisted of several weeks of career counseling and the preparation of his resume. The counselor's evaluation and follow-up meetings uncovered a strong interest in acting and directing, both of which Sidney had pursued as a hobby for the previous 25 years—with both community and religious theater groups.

As his counselor pointed out, Sidney needed "permission" (in a psychological sense) to strike out on his new career course, which took the form of the counselor's encouragement. He prepared a resume pointed in this direction, but—leaving nothing to chance—a second version geared toward his profession as a buyer. (The two versions appear on pages 159 and 160.)

After an understandably slow start, Sidney made almost as much money in his first year acting and directing as he had as a buyer. And in his second year he made considerably more. "So where were you 35 years ago when I needed you," he said to his counselor only partly in jest.

Although it was Sidney's job loss that forced him to consider this degree of change, he may not have followed through without the encouragement he received. The point is that now he was earning good money doing something he had wanted to do all his life, and was doing it well—a goal most of us would like to reach.

PROFILE: "Josephine McGinnis," co-owner with her husband of a successful convenience store in a Massachusetts city, reluctantly decided to give up their business after several robberies at gunpoint convinced them their lives were more important than their livelihoods. She decided that being a crack pistol shot was not the career skill she wanted to emphasize in job interviews.

Complicating her situation was the fact that various allergies restricted the number of places in which she could live, work, and stay healthy.

Josephine had handled the business end of their operation effectively, including all record keeping, accounting, and cash-flow management. She had a number of business-oriented computer skills. For these reasons she thought that an office manager job would be ideal for her.

The resume Josephine prepared stressed her business management experience, as well as her computer skills. After several networking interviews, she determined that her prospects would be

DIRECTOR/ACTOR

SIDNEY HAWKES
25 Harriet Drive, Whippany, NJ   07693
Service: (201) 792-4683   Home: (201) 418-9718

PROFESSIONAL QUALIFICATIONS AND PROFILE

Extensive Directing/Acting - experience in all aspects of stage crafts, including set design, lighting, makeup and theatre management:

* Teaching theatre improvisation and scene auditioning.

* Performing in more than 45 full productions.

* Directing and staging more than 25 full productions (drama and musical comedy).

* Singing, instructing, stage managing; adept at foreign accents.

EDUCATION

THE NEW SCHOOL, New York, NY Dramatic Workshop and Technical Institute
(2 years - graduate certificate)

RUTGERS UNIVERSITY, New Brunswick, NJ
Coursework concentration in English and English literature

DREW UNIVERSITY, Madison, NJ (3 mos. course) Directing Modern Theatre

EXPERIENCE - ACTING

Off-Broadway - The Burning Bush - The Miser - Emil and the Detectives

Summer Stock - Home of the Brave - The Milky Way

Regional - Drama and Musicals with: The City Lights Masquers - Center Players - The Producing Guild - New Haven Repertory Theatre - The Musical Theatre Guild

Voice-Overs/Character Voices - Kentucky Fried Chicken - Reins' New York Deli

Industrial/Commercial - The Loft (Channel 6 Newark) - CBS Pension - Vermont Federal Savings - Providence Bank and Trust

EXPERIENCE - DIRECTING

The Players Co. - New York, NY
Center Players - Brooklyn Heights, NY
City Lights Masquers - Summit, NJ

INTERESTS

Classical music, singing, travel

AWARDS

Moss Hart Memorial Award (New England Theatre Conference Direction) -
Death Trap - New Haven Repertory - 1984-1985
Hawley Cup Award - City Lights Masquers - The Price - 1973
Hawley Cup Award - City Lights Masquers - Little Foxes - 1972

SIDNEY HAWKES
25 Harriet Drive, Whippany, NJ   07693
Service: (201) 792-4683   Home: (201) 418-9718

PROFESSIONAL PROFILE

Extensive Senior Buyer experience:

* Purchasing merchandise for major retail companies (extremely
  knowledgeable in all aspects of the linens and domestics market)

* Coordinating liaison activities between merchandising and advertising

* Researching and traveling the Far East extensively to design products
  and purchase items for U.S. consumption

* Interacting with store field operations, accounts payable, training
  and development

EXPERIENCE

HILLS DEPARTMENT STORES, Canton, MA   1972 - present

THREE D DEPARTMENTS, INC., Irvine, CA 1952-1972
(formerly Fabrics National Inc.)

EDUCATION

THE NEW SCHOOL, New York, NY. Dramatic Workshops and Technical Institute
(2 years - graduate certificate)

RUTGERS UNIVERSITY, New Brunswick, NJ. Coursework concentration in
                    English and English Literature

MILITARY

United States Army - Honorable Discharge (information/education
                     specialist)

COMMUNITY ACTIVITIES

Farmington Valley Jewish Congregation, past president, religious
  committee chairman, teacher, cantor.
Boston Curtain and Drapery Club, member.
New England Theatre Conference, member.
New Haven Repertory Theatre, director, teacher.
City Lights Masquers, director, play reading committee member.
Center Players, director.
Nutmeg Players, director.
"Poetry and Play Readings Group," director/member.

greater in a small company than a large one. From her library research she targeted 37 manufacturing and service companies that were right for her, all with fewer than 100 employees.

Over a three-day period she was able to speak with the president's secretary in 28 of the companies. At 24 of these she received no encouragement for immediate employment; six of them, however, asked her to send a resume and call again in three to six months. She set up three interviews, one of which resulted in a second interview and ultimately a job offer. Josephine declined the job when she was offered less money than she made in the convenience store, with no prospects of a raise to a more suitable salary for at least a year.

Four months later, during a series of calls to the six companies that had asked her to get back to them, she was invited in to discuss an office manager's opening less than a week old and landed the job. Josephine had successfully tapped "the hidden job market." Her resume appears on page 158.

PROFILE: "Lois Springer" was an energetic, 63-year-old educator facing mandatory retirement from her school system who had no intention of stopping work. She had a high profile in the community, was politically active, but had absolutely no idea what she wanted to do.

Through career counseling, Lois tapped into a number of entrepreneurial tendencies and interests. She had run for and held office in a number of organizations, held political office in her community, and assisted in the political campaigns of candidates at the state level. Not until she reviewed this information with her counselor did she realize how important a part of her life this was.

Together they decided that as an educational consultant she could utilize all of her background and professional skills, as well as tap into her interests and abilities in community and political action. Lois researched the status of several school systems nearby, and realized that her background was ideal for solving a number of their problems.

She drew up and presented her proposals, and within two months contracted with a school system in the next county to provide in-service assistance to elementary school teachers having difficulty implementing a new literature program.

JOSEPHINE M. MCGINNIS

46 Shaw Street
Lebanon, New Hampshire   03766

Home Telephone
(603) 417-9821

PROFESSIONAL OBJECTIVE Creative position in office management, leading to developmental oportunities.

PROFILE Experienced business manager; proficient in Quicken, Professional Write, WordPerfect, Lotus 1-2-3, Express Publisher.

EXPERIENCE L.M.S. Incorporated. Fitzwilliam, NH   March 1989-Present
Owner - Manager
* Coordinate all facets of retail establishment with gross sales of over $1 million per year; choose and acquire product lines for retail sales
* Supervise bookkeeping, payroll, and regular contact with accountants
* Responsible for cash receipt control and cash flow management
* Supervise and train employees
* Design floor layouts and merchandising displays; coordinate customer and public relations

MEMORIAL HOSPITAL, Lebanon, CT   July 1982-Oct. 1989
Child Life Therapist
* Created and implemented the Adolescent Unit at Memorial Hospital; coordinated patient activities and schoolwork
* Facilitated relationships between families and hospital staff; (Position required broad general knowledge of all aspects of hospital procedures)
* Clarified information about specific procedures for patients and parents

OTHER EXPERIENCE SCHOOL OF SWIMMING, Concord, NH   Summers, 1978-81
Lifeguard and Swimming Instructor (To defray college expenses)

COMMUNITY ACTIVITIES HUNTINGTON UNITED METHODIST CHURCH   1993 - present
Senior High Youth Advisor 1994 - present, **Membership and Evangelism** work area chairperson 1994, Strawberry Festival **Co-chairperson** 1993, Administrative Council (local Church Government) 1994 to present.
NATIONAL AUDUBON SOCIETY member, CROP walk-a-thon participant for inner-city hunger (1977-present)

EDUCATION WHEELOCK COLLEGE, Boston, MA   Sept. 1978-May 1982
Bachelor of Science - Sociology/Gerontology
(G.P.A. = 3.5)

INTERESTS Skiing, swimming, gardening, theater and travel

162

Lois is currently under contract to several school systems, as well as to her state board of education. One innovative program she has marketed to two school systems is a way of making teachers more politically active, to get them more involved in the community and bring about positive change for education. So even in "retirement," Lois continues to be an agent for change.

PROFILE: "James Hare" was a 30-year-old automobile mechanic who had been fired from one job and laid off from a second in less than two years. His job loss had nothing to do with the quality of his work; he was an excellent mechanic.

The problem was that James was an independent thinker, and independent thinking automobile mechanics frequently don't do well working for dealerships. When the policy manual specifies .5 hours for a task subsequently complicated by an unforeseen problem, spending .6 hours *to do the job right* is unacceptable.

The reality was that creative, problem-solving attitudes were not positively reinforced by James's two employers; as the saying goes, only "if he went along would he get along." In essence, a strong need to get the job right the first time was the root cause of James' two terminations.

James was unsure about looking for another job—for good reason. He dreaded the thought of going through such a demeaning experience yet a third time; and even if not, employers would take a hard look at James' candidacy with the track record he owned.

As a result of some interest testing and career personality assessment, James determined that the work environment he was used to was entirely wrong for him. He was the type of person who would thrive in a more entrepreneurial atmosphere. The test results also indicated that he could be a good teacher.

Through a loan and a modest savings account, James was able to buy a small garage that he got up and running, but was not entirely comfortable with. The location was not the greatest, and James ran into insurance problems the first year. But something was missing: It turned out that he was not a pure entrepreneur—or perhaps he struck out on his own without enough maturity to reinforce the decision.

James recast his resume for instructional possibilities. With his counselor's help he rehearsed and role-played interviews in which his two terminations and failed business were sure to be asked about, until he could successfully neutralize those objections and bring the conversation around to his ability to teach fledgling mechanics.

James is now an instructor of mechanics, certified for both foreign and domestic cars.

PROFILE: Until he was let go by his publisher-employer in 1990, "Peter McDonald" had enjoyed a successful career in corporate human resource management. Since that time he has crossed an important psychological barrier. When he's asked: "What do you do?" he no longer answers in terms of past job descriptions, but in terms of current assignments with corporate clients.

Peter has not given up looking for a conventional human resource position, but he has adopted a more flexible strategy—by learning to go where the professional action is. He has several part-time positions and projects with growing firms, any one of which may lead to something permanent. These assignments provide sufficient income to keep his savings account intact and at the same time avoid taking the wrong full-time job out of panic and desperation.

Meanwhile, Peter has prepared three resumes, each reflecting one of his functional strengths, namely:

- Compensation and benefits
- Employee relations
- Training and development

Most jobs he reads or hears about are generalist positions or correspond to one of his three specialities. For generalist positions he uses his consultant's resume or rewrites whatever specialist resume is most applicable.

The first three of Peter's resumes (see pages 165–170) are geared to the areas highlighted above. Notice how the Objective, Summary, and Experience sections of each are positioned for each of these specialities, including the sequence of entries of early positions appearing on the second pages of all resumes.

For consulting positions, Peter includes the fourth version of his resume (pages 171–172), which requires neither an Objective nor a Summary because his current experience tells it all.

PETER McDONALD

186 Boston Post Road
Greenwich, CT 06830
(203) 661-1186

OBJECTIVE
Vice President, Director Compensation and Employee Benefits

SUMMARY
Design, implement and administer exempt and non-exempt compensation programs, as well as qualified and non-qualified benefit programs.

McDONALD ASSOCIATES   **1990-Present**
Human resources consulting:

- Upgraded Human Resource function from recruitment only to employee relations, compensation and employee benefit administration. Renegotiated all insurance plans, including hospital, major medical and life; established HMO coverages and 401(K) program.

- Redesigned over 100 hourly wage programs to a uniform national professional salary system for 20,000 employees in 100+ distributional centers.

- Controlled costs of annual salary adjustments by limiting annual departmental merit budgets to the cost of living. Trained supervisors to calculate departmental budgets and individual salary adjustments.

- Rationalized wage costs for sales support employees by including them in a sales incentive system based on annual revenue and margin targets rather than on increased base salaries.

- Improved employee performance by implementing a task-oriented appraisal system. Worked with general managers to develop the approach and support materials for their managers. Trained managers to evaluate performance of each job task-component, and to communicate this information to improve individual performance. Evaluations then formed the basis for subsequent merit salary adjustments.

- Conducted entrepreneurial training for 50 plant managers who were assuming profit and loss responsibilities as part of a national restructuring.

INTERNATIONAL PUBLICATIONS   **1980-1990**
VP Employee Relations   1985-1990

Responsible for enhancement of productivity and maintenance of work force flexibility in 50 subsidiaries.

- Member of merger and acquisition team:
    - analyzed compensation, benefit costs and all other personnel liabilities
    - established local personnel administration, reducing costs by 10%.

- Supervised 25 employee attitude surveys and audits:
    - improved process by graphically reporting statistical results
    - recommended specific actions for local management
    - provided follow-up training and development.

Director Human Resources, Magazine Division   1980-1985

Reported to President. Member of Senior Management Committee. Responsible for compensation, staff planning, recruitment, employee relations, organizational development, management education and sales training for this 1000 employee division. Managed corporate staff of 10 professionals and five group staffs of about same size.

INTERNATIONAL PUBLICATIONS (Continued)

- Redeployed work force from southern Connecticut location to less expensive labor markets:
    - defined new organization structure
    - assessed all experienced managers
    - down-sized management by 20%, retaining high performance personnel for basic business and new ventures
    - recruited new editorial forces in Florida and Texas.

- Rewrote compensation manual. Regraded all sales and management positions. Administered compensation policies.

- Reduced headquarters training and regional personnel costs. Savings: $700,000 annually.

- Reduced training and turnover costs by improving quality of sales recruits through targeted advertising and structured interviews.

- Increased productivity of middle managers and experienced sales personnel with result-oriented training and seminars.

FAIRFIELD PUBLICATIONS	**1970-1980**
Director of Executive Development	1975-1980
Manager of Management Development	1970-1975

- Designed and implemented communication programs for four major employee benefit changes. Trained operating unit personnel managers so they could explain and administer benefit programs at their unit level.

- Managed professional compensation program.

- Established Corporate Center for Management Development by consolidating existing divisional programs. Increased participation by 20%; reduced total expense by 10%.

- Established executive development by working directly with operating presidents to increase inter-divisional transfers and promotions. Reduced executive search fees by 40%.

EDUCATION
Fairfield University - MBA, Marketing and Human Relations, 1970.
St. John's College - BA, Economics, 1968.

PROFESSIONAL ASSOCIATIONS
American Compensation Association
American Society of Personnel Administration
American Society for Training & Development
Association of Corporate and Professional Recruiters
Human Resources Planning Society

PETER McDONALD

186 Boston Post Road
Greenwich, CT 06830
(203) 661-1186

OBJECTIVE
Vice President, Director Employee Relations

SUMMARY
Design and implement all aspects of a union-free work environment.

McDONALD ASSOCIATES   **1990-Present**
Human resources consulting:

- Redesigned over 100 hourly wage programs to a uniform national professional salary system for 20,000 employees in 100+ distributional centers. New program competes favorably with bargaining unit plan for other 40,000 employees.

- Upgraded Human Resource function from recruitment only to union-free employee relations, compensation and employee benefit administration.

- Controlled costs of annual salary adjustments by limiting annual departmental merit budgets to the cost of living. Trained supervisors to calculate departmental budgets and individual salary adjustments.

- Improved employee performance by implementing a task-oriented appraisal system. Worked with general managers to develop the approach and support materials for their managers. Trained managers to evaluate performance of each job task-component, and to communicate this information to improve individual performance. Evaluations then formed the basis for subsequent merit salary adjustments.

- Rationalized wage costs for sales support employees by including them in a sales incentive system based on annual revenue and margin targets rather than on increased base salaries.

- Conducted entrepreneurial training for 50 plant managers who were assuming profit and loss responsibilities as part of a national restructuring.

INTERNATIONAL PUBLICATIONS   **1980-1990**
VP Employee Relations   **1985-1990**

Responsible for enhancement of productivity and maintenance of work force flexibility in 50 subsidiaries.

- Defeated unionization attempt in a mid-western subsidiary and decertified a local union in California operation unit.

- Supervised 25 employee attitude surveys and audits:
    - improved process by graphically reporting statistical results
    - recommended specific actions for local management
    - provided follow-up training and development.

- Member of merger and acquisition team:
    - analyzed compensation, benefit costs and all other personnel liabilities
    - established local personnel administration, reducing costs by 10%.

INTERNATIONAL PUBLICATIONS (Continued)
Director Human Resources, Magazine Division   1980-1985

Reported to President. Member of Senior Management Committee. Responsible for maintenance of union-free employee relations, staff planning, recruitment, compensation, sales training, organizational development and management education of this 1000 employee division. Managed corporate staff of 10 professionals and five group staffs of about same size.

- Redeployed work force from southern Connecticut location to less expensive labor markets:
  - defined new organization structure
  - assessed all experienced managers
  - down-sized management by 20%, retaining high performance personnel for basic business and new ventures
  - recruited new editorial forces in Florida and Texas.
- Reduced training and turnover costs by improving quality of sales recruits through targeted advertising and structured interviews.
- Increased productivity of middle managers and experienced sales personnel with result-oriented training and seminars.
- Reduced headquarters training and regional personnel costs. Savings: $700,000 annually.
- Rewrote compensation manual. Regraded all sales and management positions. Administered compensation policies.

FAIRFIELD PUBLICATIONS   **1970-1980**
Director of Executive Development   1975-1980
Manager of Management Development   1970-1975

- Helped defeat unionization attempts in Bridgeport, CT, New York City and Philadelphia.
- Designed and implemented communication programs for four major employee benefit changes. Trained personnel managers so they could explain and administer the program, thereby maintaining direct communication with employees.
- Established executive development by working directly with operating presidents to increase inter-divisional transfers and promotions. Reduced executive search fees by 40%.
- Established Corporate Center for Management Development by consolidating existing divisional programs. Increased participation by 20%; reduced total expense by 10%.
- Managed professional compensation program.

EDUCATION
Fairfield University - MBA, Marketing and Human Relations, 1970.
St. John's College - BA, Economics, 1968.

PROFESSIONAL ASSOCIATIONS
American Compensation Association
American Society of Personnel Administration
American Society for Training & Development
Association of Corporate and Professional Recruiters
Human Resources Planning Society

PETER McDONALD

186 Boston Post Road
Greenwich, CT 06830
(203) 661-1186

OBJECTIVE
Vice President, Director of Training and Development

SUMMARY
Design and deliver development programs for executives, managers, sales and sales support staff.

McDONALD ASSOCIATES   **1990-Present**
Human resources consulting:

- Conducted entrepreneurial training for 50 plant managers who were assuming profit and loss responsibilities as part of a national restructuring.

- Improved employee performance by implementing a task-oriented appraisal system. Worked with general managers to develop the approach and support materials for their managers. Trained managers to evaluate performance of each job task-component, and to communicate this information to improve individual performance. Evaluations then formed the basis for subsequent merit salary adjustments.

- Controlled costs of annual salary adjustments by limiting annual departmental merit budgets to the cost of living. Trained supervisors to calculate departmental budgets and individual salary adjustments.

- Redesigned over 100 hourly wage programs to a uniform national professional salary system for 20,000 employees in 100+ distributional centers.

- Rationalized wage costs for sales support employees by including them in a sales incentive system based on annual revenue and margin targets rather than on increased base salaries.

- Upgraded Human Resource function from recruitment only to employee relations, compensation and employee benefit administration.

INTERNATIONAL PUBLICATIONS   **1980-1990**
VP Employee Relations   **1985-1990**

Responsible for enhancement of productivity and maintenance of work force flexibility in 50 subsidiaries.

- Supervised 25 employee attitude surveys and audits:
    - provided follow-up training and development
    - improved survey process by graphically reporting statistical results
    - recommended specific actions for local management.

- Member of merger and acquisition team:
    - analyzed compensation, benefit costs and all other personnel liabilities
    - established local personnel administration, reducing costs by 10%.

Director Human Resources, Magazine Division   **1980-1985**

Reported to President. Member of Senior Management Committee. Responsible for organizational development, management education, sales training, staff planning, recruitment, employee relations and compensation for this 1000 employee division. Managed corporate staff of 10 professionals and five group staffs of about same size.

INTERNATIONAL PUBLICATIONS (Continued)

- Increased productivity of middle managers and experienced sales personnel with result-oriented training and seminars.

- Restructured headquarters training, eliminating duplicative local training. Savings: $700,000 annually.

- Reduced training and turnover costs by improving quality of sales recruits through targeted advertising and structured interviews.

- Rewrote compensation manual. Regraded all sales and management positions. Administered compensation policies.

- Redeployed work force from southern Connecticut location to less expensive labor markets:
    - defined new organization structure
    - assessed all experienced managers
    - down-sized management by 20%, retaining high performance personnel for basic business and new ventures
    - recruited new editorial forces in Florida and Texas.

FAIRFIELD PUBLICATIONS 1970-1980
Director of Executive Development 1975-1980
Manager of Management Development 1970-1975

- Established Corporate Center for Management Development by consolidating existing divisional programs. Increased participation by 20%; reduced total expense by 10%.

- Established executive development by working directly with operating presidents to increase inter-divisional transfers and promotions. Reduced executive search fees by 40%.

- Designed and implemented communication programs for four major employee benefit changes. Trained all operating unit personnel managers to explain and administer benefit programs.

- Managed professional compensation program.

EDUCATION
Fairfield University - MBA, Marketing and Human Relations, 1970.
St. John's College - BA, Economics, 1968.

PROFESSIONAL ASSOCIATIONS
American Compensation Association
American Society of Personnel Administration
American Society for Training & Development
Association of Corporate and Professional Recruiters
Human Resources Planning Society

PETER McDONALD

186 Boston Post Road
Greenwich, CT 06830
(203) 661-1186

McDONALD ASSOCIATES   1990-Present
Human resources consulting:

Human resource consulting with emphasis in: compensation and employee benefit design and administration; employee relations; training and development. Current clients include: International Distributors, a multi-plant national manufacturer and a number of Wall Street financial institutions.

- Redesigned over 100 hourly wage programs to a uniform national professional salary system for 20,000 employees in 100+ distributional centers.

- Controlled costs of annual salary adjustments by limiting annual departmental merit budgets to the cost of living. Trained supervisors to calculate departmental budgets and individual salary adjustments.

- Improved employee performance by implementing a task-oriented appraisal system. Worked with general managers to develop the approach and support materials for their managers. Trained managers to evaluate performance of each job task-component, and to communicate this information to improve individual performance. Evaluations then formed the basis for subsequent merit salary adjustments.

- Rationalized wage costs for sales support employees by including them in a sales incentive system based on annual revenue and margin targets rather than on increased base salaries.

- Upgraded Human Resource function from recruitment only to employee relations, compensation and employee benefit administration.

- Conducted entrepreneurial training for plant managers who were assuming profit and loss responsibilities as part of a restructuring.

INTERNATIONAL PUBLICATIONS   1980-1990
VP Employee Relations   1985-1990

Responsible for enhancement of productivity and maintenance of work force flexibility in 50 subsidiaries.

- Supervised 25 employee attitude surveys and audits:
    - improved process by graphically reporting statistical results
    - recommended specific actions for local management
    - provided follow-up training and development

- Member of merger and acquisition team:
    - analyzed compensation, benefit costs and all other personnel liabilities
    - established local personnel administration, reducing costs by 10%.

Director Human Resources, Magazine Division   1980-1985

Reported to President. Member of Senior Management Committee. Responsible for staff planning, recruitment, employee relations, compensation, sales training, organizational development and management education of this 1000 employee division. Managed corporate staff of 10 professionals and five group staffs of about same size.

INTERNATIONAL PUBLICATIONS (Continued)

- Redeployed work force from southern Connecticut location to less expensive labor markets:
    - defined new organization structure
    - assessed all experienced managers
    - down-sized management by 20%, retaining high performance personnel for basic business and new ventures
    - recruited new editorial forces in Florida and Texas.

- Reduced training and turnover costs by improving quality of sales recruits through targeted advertising and structured interviews.

- Increased productivity of middle managers and experienced sales personnel with result-oriented training and seminars.

- Reduced headquarters training and regional personnel costs. Savings: $700,000 annually.

- Rewrote compensation manual. Regraded all sales and management positions. Administered compensation policies.

FAIRFIELD PUBLICATIONS   **1970-1980**
Director of Executive Development   1975-1980
Manager of Management Development   1970-1975

- Established executive development by working directly with operating presidents to increase inter-divisional transfers and promotions. Reduced executive search fees by 40%.

- Managed professional compensation program.

- Established Corporate Center for Management Development by consolidating existing divisional programs. Increased participation by 20%; reduced total expense by 10%.

- Designed and implemented communication programs for four major employee benefit changes.

EDUCATION
Fairfield University - MBA, Marketing and Human Relations, 1970.
St. John's College - BA, Economics, 1968.

PROFESSIONAL ASSOCIATIONS
American Compensation Association
American Society of Personnel Administration
American Society for Training & Development
Association of Corporate and Professional Recruiters
Human Resources Planning Society

PROFILE: "John Nicholson" owned an extremely successful sales and marketing record in the adhesives business; but when his boss came to the conclusion that John represented a real threat to the boss's advancement, he found a way to get rid of him by consolidating two regions and "downsizing" him.

John had no thought of leaving the industry. It was all he knew and wanted. He decided to direct his campaign purely in adhesives, until such time as was obvious that he couldn't get the job he wanted.

He decided to exploit two of his strongest advantages: an unparalleled professional record, and his network. Within three months John was offered a job with a direct competitor of his former company, paying 25 percent more than his last job. In addition to his resume, John used powerful sales letters and a one-page compilation of his record in the industry. On pages 174 and 175 is the letter that got him an interview with Hanratty Adhesives, which three weeks later led to a job offer.

PROFILE: "Jill Lockhart" had grown up in a very traditional family. Her mother stayed home with the children while Dad provided the income. Jill in turn was nine years into a traditional marriage of her own, and had planned to be at home for her children as they grew up.

When her husband's corporate career ended suddenly through a massive downsizing, Jill was shocked. Subsequently he was able to get two part-time jobs, but the money coming in was not enough to make the mortgage and other expenses.

Jill decided that it was time to get a job to supplement the family paycheck. Actually, there was no alternative. After solving the problems of daycare for the three children, Jill prepared the resume on page 179. Her part-time position with Regent Relocation had given her valuable skills and accomplishments, but ended when the company moved two years previously. Jersey Galleries was operated out of a friend's two-car garage. The assistant teacher's position had been unpaid, but enabled the children to attend nursery school tuition-free.

With this resume and a job-search campaign centered in the immediate area, Jill was able to find a full-time benefits counselor position with a third-party vendor just 15 minutes from home.

October 21, 1994

Mr. Robert Ackerman
President
Hanratty Adhesives Corporation
46 Billings Street
Sharon, MA   07418

Dear Mr. Ackerman:

Your ad in the October 14, 1994 <u>Wall Street Journal</u> could have been written
specifically with me in mind. Over the past 20 years I have built a
distinguished career in the sales and marketing of adhesives for the
nonwoven disposables and tape and label industries. I also have developed a
large number of professional relationships that last to this day, including
many individuals who can attest to the accuracy of this letter and
accompanying resume.

Let me address the principal requirements for your Director of Marketing and
Sales position:

*   **Significant, solid sales track record**
    I offer 20 years of unparalleled adhesives industry sales and marketing
    experience, including the growth of a personal products line from $60,000
    to $7 million in four years (see attached record of achievements).

*   **Well-established personal relationships with many potential customers**
    I can discuss in considerable detail my close relationships with key
    executives at companies such as Kline-Smith (Sam Johnson), Terrance &
    Terrance (Pete Karon), Pope & Poppins (Jill Selleck) and Tarkenton (Ross
    Raymond), to mention a few.

*   **In-depth understanding of the markets**
    My on-the-job experience, as well as my participation as moderator at
    Insight conferences, has kept me abreast of all applicable market
    situations.

*   **Ability to provide corporate direction for new product development**
    In various situations over the course of my tenure at Anderson Eckardt,
    particularly as Business Manager of Nonwovens, I set the corporate
    direction for product development (including the decision to bring Stik-
    r-Tape to the marketplace for Kline-Smith and Jones & Salyers after four
    years of product testing and development)

*   **Excellent communication skills**
    There are two kinds of communication at which I excel -- verbal
    communication and communication as a management tool. Examples in each
    area are:

1) I have written numerous strategic business plans that have led to
    successful sales penetration in nonwoven markets, and will be happy to
    provide nonproprietary examples upon request;

2) My management style is to clearly communicate corporate and departmental
    missions to all individuals reporting to me, and to similarly listen
    carefully to my employees. This philosophy has resulted in effective
    performance by my subordinates, and virtually no turnover of employees
    personally hired by me.

174

*   **Profit and loss responsibility**
    I have held profit and loss responsibility in three of my last four
    positions: 1) as District Manager at Anderson Eckardt, managing both
    sales and manufacturing; 2) as Business Manager at Anderson; and 3) as
    Regional Manager at Felkar with P&L responsibility for manufacturing and
    sales in the northeast region. As General Manager for a joint venture in
    1987 I had complete P&L responsibility (see attached resume for details).

I look forward to discussing with you in person each of the above
requirements, as well as other aspects of the position. I consider myself a
problem solver for any combination of circumstances that might occur, and
will gladly accept any test you might devise that will cause you to view me
the same way.

Sincerely,

John S. Nicholson
Enclosures

JOHN S. NICHOLSON
1810 Tamiani Trail
Joliet, IL   60191
(708) 934-8661 (Office)
(708) 663-1172 (Home)

SUMMARY: Sales/marketing executive with 20 successful years adhesive industry
experience. Exemplary record of customer retention, while
consistently exceeding revenue and growth goals. Extensive plant-
level profit and loss responsibility. Skilled and motivational
manager with virtually no turnover of employees personally hired.
Strong background in strategic planning.

EXPERIENCE: FELKAR ADHESIVES, La Grange, IL
(A Division of Manchester Chemicals, Inc.)
Northeast Regional Manager

1990 to
Present

* Direct marketing and sales operations of 13-state region,
  supervising eight sales representatives and four support people

* Turned around stagnant region with no growth in preceding six
  years to increase revenues by 37% ($6.5 million to $9 million)
  over three-year period, utilizing innovative marketing techniques
  and restructuring sales operation (see attached sheet for year-by-
  year performance record)

* Supervised operations of 35-employee West Haven manufacturing
  facility (in addition to current responsibilities) for two years
  before regional reorganization

1984 to
1990

CANIFER STICKY STUFF, Mt. Hope, NJ
General Manager

* Set up joint ventures between U.S./Belgian adhesive companies,
  including business plan, pro formas, funding strategies and
  physical plant design

1974 to
1989

ANDERSON ECKARDT COMPANY, Sandusky, OH
National Account Manager   (1987)
Business Manager   (1982-86)
District Manager   (1978-81)
Sales Representative   (1972-77)

* Fifteen years of consistent contributions to corporate revenue and
  profit growth, resulting in three promotions to positions of
  increasing responsibility

  - Held profit-and-loss responsibility for discrete business
    units over a five-year period, both as Business Manager and as
    National Account Manager

  - Responsible for dramatic sales and profit increases 14 out of 15
    years (see attached sheets for year-by-year performance record),
    including doubling sales in four-year period, and growing one
    account from $60,000 to $7 million over same period of time

176

1972-1974   OLIVER INTERNATIONAL CORPORATION, Phoenix, AZ
             Sales Representative

             * Met all sales goals

1970-1972   FUJI COLOR AND CHEMICAL
             Sales Representative

             * Met all sales goals

1969-1970   ENDICOTT PAPER COMPANY
             Sales Representative

             * Met all sales goals

EDUCATION: AMHERST COLLEGE, Amherst, MA
             1968 - B.A., Economics and Sociology

JOHN S. NICHOLSON

Selected Professional Accomplishments

<u>ANDERSON ECKARDT</u>

1974-1979	As sales representative, met goals five consecutive years
1980	District Manager: 19.2% sales increase (ranked 4th out of 23 districts)*
1981	District Manager: 26.5% sales increase (ranked 1st out of 23 districts)
1982	District Manager: 17.2% sales increase (ranked 7th out of 22 districts)
1983	District Manager: 13.2% sales increase (ranked 6th out of 22 districts)
1980-83	(Simultaneously held plant management responsibility; exceeded net profit budget all three years)
1984	Non-Woven Business Manager: 20.8% sales increase; (1st out of 13 business units)
1986	Non-Woven Business Manager: 28.8% sales increase; (3rd out of 13 business units)
1987	Non-Woven Business Manager: 11% sales decrease; (5th out of 7 business units)
1988	Non-Woven Business Manager and National Account Manager: 26% sales increase (3rd out of 5 business units)
1984-1988	(Also far exceeded net profit goals 4 out of 5 years)

<u>FELKAR ADHESIVES</u>

1991	Northeast Regional Manager and Plant Manager: 13% increase in pounds; 22% increase in sales; 19% increase in gross margin
1992	Northeast Regional Manager and Plant Manager: 10% increase in pounds; 6% increase in sales; 5% increase in gross margin (gross margin at 33.5% was highest of 6 regions; profit as a percentage of net sales was 26.5%)
1993	Northeast Regional Manager: Currently 13% ahead in pounds; 10.5% ahead in sales; 8% ahead in gross margin

---

* Computer printouts available to substantiate all percentages

JILL LOCKHART
22 Smith Place
Green Bank, NJ 07894
201-875-1907

OBJECTIVE: Chief Administrative Manager; Office Manager

SUMMARY: Experience combines customer services and relations, as well as purchasing and distribution in diverse business environments.

1989-1993   **Regent Relocation Management** - Ft. Lee, NJ

Acquisition Coordinator: ordered, evaluated and assessed property appraisals, real estate broker opinions, home inspections and legal/title opinions to aid in determining value for transferred executives' properties.

Client Services Coordinator: supported Relocation counselors in contacts with transferring employees; identified sources of appraisers, brokers and attorneys; ordered all inspections, monitored receipt of reports, and researched problems; aided in calculating transferee's equity and processed payments to facilitate property buy-out.

Relocation Secretary: provided direct administrative support to Client Services Director and Manager. Promoted to newly-created Client Services Coordinator position.

1985-1989   **Jersey Galleries, Ltd.** - Green Bank, NJ

Partner in children's clothing mail order business: order fulfillment; customer service; accounts payable and receivable; inventory maintenance; and computerized customer listings. The business sold at 100% profit to original investors.

1980-1985   **Neighborhood Nursery School, Inc.** - Green Bank, NJ

Assistant Teacher: assisted Head Teacher in playschool program.

1969-1977   **NBC, The Singer Company and Pfizer International**

Administrative positions

1969-1969   B.S. - Garden State University

OTHER: Extensive use of personal computer; exposure to WordPerfect and Appleworks word processing, order entry and light bookkeeping.

PROFILE: "Melanie Bridgeman," an accomplished educational publishing marketing manager, lost her Chicago job in a corporate downsizing. Because three years remained on her husband's employment contract, however, Melanie was unable to consider job opportunities outside the metropolitan Chicago area.

Problem was, jobs in her field were scarce in Chicago. It became clear that the only viable opportunities for her were to be found in other parts of the country, so Melanie changed her strategy.

When the second executive recruiter to call Melanie in seven weeks described yet another scintillating job—on the East coast, of course—she asked him if the company would consider the possibility of her working out of Joliet, making as many New York trips as were necessary to get the job done.

"What they have in mind would seem to call for a lot of time out of the office generating business anyway," Melanie told him. "And in an era of increasing dependence on faxes and modems, I should be able to manage my other responsibilities from Joliet if just minimal day-to-day contact is involved."

The recruiter relayed Melanie's suggestion to his client, who agreed that the idea was not out of the question and asked for specifics.

Because Melanie's idea represented a new kind of working relationship to the prospective employer, she covered all aspects of the arrangement in detail—including features and benefits—in an attempt to raise the "company comfort level" as high as possible.

Beginning on page 181 are the proposal and resume Melanie developed for the position of Marketing Manager of Special Sales, and which led to her New York interview. Note in particular how Melanie not only puts forth her qualifications for the job in a forceful manner, but neutralizes as well all of the objections she can think of for conducting the job from a distance—making the case in fact that in some ways this would be a *better* way to fill this position.

PROFILE: "Charles Wheeler" grew up in Oak Brook, IL. After college he found jobs as an internal sales rep and legal assistant, which confirmed his desire to study finance at the University of Chicago School of Business. While there, in order to broaden his experience further, he served as a legal assistant and managed the closing of a major bond issue. *(Continued on page 189)*

Overview

Marketing textbooks requires a solid understanding of the targeted audience: college professors, libraries, bookstores, trainers, computer retailers. It demands an ability not only to identify and communicate the benefits of a given title, but also to translate those benefits into the particular language of that audience.

This understanding and ability is second nature to me: I have successfully marketed hundreds of texts, basal series, and supplements in the education market, as well as in alternative markets such as corporate daycare facilities, public libraries, and school supply stores. In addition, I've marketed and sold trade books in a variety of retail, special sales, and premium markets.

The purpose of this proposal is to demonstrate how my experience and capabilities match your requirements for a Marketing Manager, and show how I would carry out the responsibilities of the position.

Background

I have a strong background in all phases of educational marketing, as well as five years' experience selling books at retail and special markets. I believe these skills would transfer well to the college market, whether I am creating campaigns for new texts, repackaging or repositioning products, or developing new markets for specific titles.

- My expertise in **marketing to educators** and my own **teaching experience** give me an in-depth knowledge of the education market what educators want and how to communicate with them. This in-depth knowledge enables me to *develop creative campaigns* targeted to a particular audience.

- My background in **creating and selling trade books** has given me a strong understanding of the market for special sales, as well as the intricacies of retail selling. It is this understanding that gives me the ability to *uncover new markets* for specific titles.

- My experience in **strategic planning and product management** gives me a clear sense of the importance of product positioning, packaging, cover design, and presentation. This experience would be an asset as I *repackage or reposition* existing products.

Expertise

I've outlined the basic responsibilities in most marketing positions and indicated how I would carry them out. While the areas I've identified here are somewhat generic, with more information they could be expanded to address your needs specifically.

Creative The following four areas require conceptual and problem-solving skills, as well as strengths in planning, organizing, writing and identifying needs. Any preparation work for these areas: gathering product information, talking to field representatives, brainstorming ideas, studying the product, or communicating with the New York staff, could be handled by phone, mail, or FAX. If in-person meetings were necessary, we could plan them in such a way as to maximize everyone's time.

Marketing Campaigns My experience in start-up organizations has given me a chance to work from the ground up in creating sales and marketing campaigns that work for a particular audience. I have learned to creatively address specific goals by developing marketing strategies for dozens of single-title texts and basal series.

Writing/Communications I have conceptualized and written hundreds of proposals, collateral pieces, direct response letters, space ads, catalogs, research articles, position papers, and newsletters.

Market Research I am particularly strong in identifying market opportunities. I can analyze industry and market trends to uncover untapped markets (such as retail or special markets) or better target existing markets.

Product Management In developing books for special sales or corporate-sponsored markets, I've learned to develop, position, price, and package products for specific audiences, whether existing customers or new prospects.

Project Management Past the creative stage, most of my experience in marketing has involved managing projects or project teams—I have extensive experience directing freelancers on projects ranging from promotional packages to videos and books. With careful systems for scheduling, tracking and budgeting, and regular feedback in the form of updates or reports, communication with the New York office would be streamlined.

Resource Management Managing outside resources for writing and design requires a clear understanding of the audience, objectives, and end product. I have directed writers and designers extensively, which enables me to have a keen sense of the tone the writing should have, and the feel and look the design should take.

Tracking and Scheduling I have experience in setting up systems for tracking resources and schedule, by either using existing software or creating customized programs.

Budgeting and Financial Control Strong analytical and budgeting skills have been a strength for me in managing budgets of up to $2 million. I have the ability to direct budgets and cash flow and to provide a variety of financial reports as needed.

Benefits

More and more companies, especially those with entrepreneurial spirits, are allowing employees to work out of home offices. They're doing this not just because they can—it's true that there's almost nothing that can't be covered by phone, FAX, modem, a computerized network or electronic mail—but because there are hidden benefits, such as:

Saving moving expenses and air travel.

By not having to relocate me to New York, you could save thousands of dollars in moving expenses. In addition, any required air travel would be cheaper and more accessible from Chicago. With careful budgeting, costs for any trips to the New York office could be kept to a minimum—by flip-flopping the city of origin, I could qualify for the lowest airfares.

Expanding resources with an already-established network.

I've worked in the Chicago area for ten years and have established an extremely valuable network of writers, editors, designers, photographers, illustrators, film separators, and printers. These could be an additional, much less expensive source than New York suppliers.

A focused work setting would mean greater productivity.

Many types of work are enhanced by being done off-site. Not only are there fewer interruptions and meetings, but when people are accountable for their own time, they are naturally more productive. They also have to plan and organize more effectively the time they need with others.

I'd be available for direct and uninterrupted access by telephone.

Since working in an off-site office means fewer interruptions and meetings, I would be more easily accessible to management, staff members and sales representatives on a continual, uninterrupted basis.

Summary

I believe that my expertise in educational marketing could be a tremendous asset to your company as you expand your presence in the college textbook market. I have the knowledge and expertise needed to speak to your audience, the experience in developing new markets, and the ability to position products to sell.

MELANIE B. BRIDGEMAN
18 Lake Hill Way • Joliet, Illinois 60433 • 815/410-9297

ADDISON-WORSLEY PUBLISHING COMPANY
School Division, Kankakee, Illinois

MARKETING DIRECTOR   1988-Present

I was recruited to this major publisher as part of a newly-formed marketing group when Division sales were at $42 million. I formed a complete in-house agency for developing and directing advertising, promotion, marketing services, sales support, and product training campaigns for nine product lines, managing an annual budget of $2 million.

- **Strategic Planning:** Created strategic plans and budgets for all product lines. Developed promotional campaigns--including collateral, direct mail, catalogs, trade shows, sales support, and training materials--to launch two basal programs and more than thirty new single titles.

- **Direct Marketing:** Instituted the first direct mail program to reach more than 350,000 customers in one year. Improved timing of all mailings, customized mail pieces for lead generation or direct selling, implemented format changes that resulted in 35% savings. The first supplementary direct mail catalog generated $250,000 in sales in the first month.

- **Advertising:** Set up an in-house agency for space advertising, resulting in an annual savings of $25,000-$30,000. Improved communications with major educational publications to obtain premium advertising space.

- **Management:** Created and trained staff of five; set up network of twenty freelance employees resulting in lower overhead costs and greater productivity. Instituted systems for scheduling and project management, budget tracking, inquiry fulfillment and analysis.

- **Product Training:** Developed a consistent, unified program for sales presentations through audio tapes, video tapes, slides, flip charts, and transparencies.

MC DOUGAL, LITTELL & COMPANY
Evanston, Illinois

ADVERTISING MANAGER   1984 - 1988

In the four years I was with this publishing company, sales grew from less than $10 million to more than $23 million. I gained experience in all aspects of marketing, including pricing, sampling, product development, sales strategies, product training.

- **Product Management:** Established product positioning for collateral materials, space ads, and sales presentations.

- **Sales Support:** Introduced direct mail campaigns for lead generation that generated 20-25% response rate on the average.

- **Planning/Management:** Created and managed promotion plan for basal and supplementary titles with an annual budget of $750,000.

187

- **Trade Show Marketing:** Directed the design and construction of a new trade show booth that was custom designed to meet the needs of an el-hi publisher.

- **Special Event Marketing:** Arranged entertainment functions, special events for customer groups at all national and regional exhibits.

- **Creative:** Wrote position papers, promotional materials, front matter for Teacher's Editions, and research papers for various consultants and authors.

NATIONAL TEXTBOOK COMPANY
Lincolnwood, Illinois

ADVERTISING MANAGER   1983 - 1984

As Advertising Manager, I had complete responsibility for the budgeting and production of six annual catalogs, hundreds of brochures, sales letters, direct mail pieces, and media ads. I was promoted to this position with less than one year of experience in publishing.

COPYWRITER/ASSISTANT ADVERTISING MANAGER   1983

I wrote catalog, brochure and space ad copy, coordinated media schedule, placed ads, and promoted products through book reviews.

TAMPA COLLEGE MEDICAL EDUCATION CENTER
St. Petersburg, Florida

ENGLISH INSTRUCTOR   1982

I prepared curriculum and taught courses in English Grammar and Composition at this two-year vocational college.

EDUCATION   Graduate Study: 30 hours toward M.A. In English and linguistics, University of South Florida, 1981-1982

B.A., English, Florida Atlantic University, 1980

RELATED
EXPERIENCE   *Direct Mail Marketing Days, Chicago, 1982*
Direct Mail Marketing to the Education Market, New York, 1983
Boothsmanship Seminar, Chicago, 1984
Professional Selling Skills, Boston, 1985
Planning and Directing Performance, Monterey, 1986
Effective Supervision, University of California, San Francisco, 1986
Frontline Leadership, Zenger-Miller Training, Menlo Park, 1986
Strategies for Successful Presentations, Boston, 1987

Upon receiving his M.B.A., Charles found a job at NBC in New York, as a senior financial analyst. Unfortunately, the stock market crash of 1987 cut this job short. Because of his persistence he has found two excellent jobs since that time, either one of which could have developed into a long-term career were it not for continuing employment cutbacks in the information/financial services industry.

Charles used several strategies and resumes in his job campaign. When he realized that he would have more success looking for positions that combined aspects of both his marketing and financial services backgrounds, however, his campaign began to come together. On pages 190–191 is the version of his resume that he used for marketing/financial services opportunities:

Wheeler's letter to George Beck (see page 192) followed a call to Beck Publishing. He decided to write the president personally after getting his name from the switchboard. A week after sending the letter he followed up with a phone call, and received a return call from Beck within 10 minutes.

"Yes, I got it," Mr. Beck said. "I wish I had a job for you, but I don't. You have a background we would be interested in under different circumstances. For a start, though, come on in, and we'll give you a copy of whatever directories you might need to get a better handle on what we're doing. And while you're here, there are a few people I think you should meet."

Based on the interviews arranged by George Beck, Charles suggested two consulting projects to the vice president of marketing that were under consideration at the time this book went to press.

The president of the financial division of the Information Industry Association gave Wheeler the name of the Vice President for Marketing at Bridge Street Information, whom he knew slightly. The marketing VP passed Charles's letter (see page 193) on to his boss, who in turn forwarded it to the next-level general manager.

Human resources called Charles to arrange for a half-day of interviews, starting with them, then with the marketing VP, and then with the general manager who had wound up with Wheeler's letter. All agreed that the company was looking for a director of product development, although the job's specs had not yet been written up.

Charles L. Wheeler
20 West 17th Street, #7B New York, NY 10016
(212) 814-6409

Objective   *Marketing or business/product development position*

Summary
    Results-driven, analytical manager experienced in creating and implementing business, sales, and marketing plans. Track record of successful performance with responsibility for market research, market segmentation, customer and product classification, competitor analysis, print advertising, direct response, publicity, promotion, event marketing, pricing, profit and ROI analyses, training, and sales strategies.

    Computer literate, disciplined team player with strong written, verbal and presentation communication skills who is comfortable leading, motivating and managing others. Background spans publishing, financial services, professional services, information providers, and communications.

Experience

1991-1993   **American Financial Services,** New York, NY

Marketing Manager - Managed planning, development and marketing of $25 million product line of professional information services. Created and implemented marketing and business development strategies to achieve P&L objectives. Managed associate product manager.

- Developed and implemented new product marketing plan and managed successful product launch.
  Won Financial Industry Association Product Achievement Award, generating over $500K annualized revenues -- over $3 million projected in 2 years.

- *Created new product training program* and materials and conducted company-wide training sessions for sales and client service staff.

- Developed formal client contact program to maintain client relationships and increase ongoing business *with more than 30,000 accounts.*

- Structured and facilitated problem analysis and resolution program.
  Resulted in product quality and service improvements.

- Succeeded in repositioning unprofitable service.
  Resulted in 20% increase in penetration of profitable market segment.

1987-1991   **U.S. Financial Services,** New York, NY

Product Manger, Financial Seminars (1991) - Managed $1.2 million business unit which produced high profile conferences and published information products designed to inform the financial services community and enhance the company's image. Directed development and planning of products marketed in the U.S. and Japan. Managed two product planners.

- Created and implemented marketing strategy to generate incremental revenues through corporate sponsorships and advertising sales.

- Cultivated relationships with senior level public and private sector executives to develop market intelligence and recruit conference speakers.

Product Manager, Civic Directory (1989-1990)
Managed $1.7 million P&L responsibility for semiannual directory marketed to the securities industry. Directed all editorial, production, sales, marketing and development activities. Supervised staff of 8.

Repositioned mature product for growth -- sales, revenues, and spin-off products.
Turned around declining sales trend and achieved 10% revenue growth.

190

U.S. Financial Services, New York, NY   *(continued)*

- Initiated product redesign.

- Directed development of database publishing system and managed transition.

- Identified new market segments and expanded product scope.

- Created new marketing and sales techniques.

- Streamlined procedures to support market analysis and improve customer service.

Manager, Strategic Analysis (1987-1989)
Formulated strategies for development, launch and growth of print and electronic financial information products. *Performed investment analysis* of new products and acquisitions. Developed and managed performance tracking and reporting system.

1986-1987   **NBC Inc.**, New York, NY
Senior Financial Analyst - Developed monthly financial forecast of production activities and operating expenses. Prepared annual operating budget and analyzed monthly budget performance. Performed profit impact analysis. Interacted with executive levels in staff and line management.

1985   **Chicago Dept. of Environmental Protection**, Chicago, IL
Summer   **Analyst**, Planning Officer - Designed internal control system for Water Board expense fund.

1983-1984   **Brown & Dudley,** Chicago, IL
Legal Assistant, Municipal Law - Managed closing of 20 million dollar bond issue.

1981-1983   **Financial Forms Company**, Chicago, IL
Internal Sales Representative - Provided technical information and sales support.

Education   **University of Chicago School of Business**, Chicago, IL (1984-1986)
M.B.A., Finance

University of Chicago, Chicago, IL (1977-1981)
B.S., *Cum Laude*, Psychology.
Special project: Team research on psychological entrapment.

American Scandinavian Fellowship, Upsala, Sweden (1980, Spring)
Researched organization and strategic characteristics of multinational firms.

April 20, 1993

Mr. George Beck
President
Beck Publishing
100 Lexington Avenue, 2nd Floor
New York, NY 10011

Dear Mr. Beck:

I am familiar with some of the directories published by Beck and know them to have an excellent reputation. I have nearly seven years of marketing, product development and business development experience in the finance and publishing industry since earning my M.B.A. at the University of Chicago School of Business. I am now seeking a new position in a small to medium-sized company and believe my skills could be of benefit to Beck Publishing.

My strong marketing skills and ability to develop and implement business strategies have resulted in a successful track record of performance in tough operating environments. My background is further described on the enclosed resume. At U.S. Financial Services I took on the role of product champion for a semi-annual directory and data base product. My ability to identify market opportunities was key as I redefined a mature product and successfully implemented a strategy to generate new business. Subsequently at American Financial Services, I developed and implemented a new product marketing plan and managed the introduction of a customized information service. This new service is a departure from the company's traditional "commoditized" products and has won a Financial Industry Association *Achievement Award.*

My strong interpersonal skills and creative thinking have been assets in a challenging business environment. I would like to learn more about Beck Publishing and to explore how my skills and experience could benefit your company. I would appreciate the opportunity to meet with you, and will call your office next week.

Sincerely,

Charles L. Wheeler

Over the next several weeks, Charles was able to put together a complete picture of the company's needs for this position, and after three more interviews accepted the job.

July 21, 1993

Mr. J. Markham Jackson
Vice President, Marketing
Bridge Street Information Corp.
150 Bridge Street, 9th Floor
New York, NY 10005

Dear Mr. Jackson:

I am writing to you at the suggestion of Knowlton Phillips, the immediate past chair of the board of the Financial Industry Association. I have seven years of marketing and business development experience in the financial and legal industries since earning my M.B.A. at the University of Chicago School of Business. I am now seeking a new position and would appreciate your help identifying opportunities with Bridge Street Information or elsewhere in the industry.

My product management skills and my ability to develop and implement business strategies have resulted in a successful track record of performance in tough operating environments. At American Financial Services, I developed and implemented a new product marketing plan and managed the introduction of a customized information service. This new service was a departure from the company's traditional "commoditized" products and won a Financial Industry Association's *Achievement Award*.

At U.S. Financial Service, I took on the challenge of an inflexible, mature product in a contracting market. I identified a market opportunity and developed a strategy to position this directory and data base product in an expanded marketplace. Driving this strategy to generate new business took my leadership in managing people and limited resources. My background is further described on the enclosed resume.

My strong analytical skills, interpersonal skills and creative thinking have been assets in a challenging business environment. I would appreciate your suggestions for identifying opportunities and would like to meet with you at your convenience. I'll call you in a few days.

Sincerely,

Charles L. Wheeler

PROFILE: "Eric Nelson" was 34, married, and miserable in a job for a research and development firm that had represented a promotion for him, and that had offered opportunities his former employer could not match. Many of the promises made by management at his new company did not materialize, however. A promotion assured him within a year was delayed twice—and never referred to again. Moreover, Eric had reason to believe that some of his new company's dealings were unethical.

In broadening his network for a new job search, Eric contacted his former employer, with whom he continued to enjoy a good relationship. In fact, he and his old boss usually had lunch at least once a year to touch base, both professionally and personally.

As it happened, his old company had prospered since Eric's departure. A small consulting company they had acquired was in need of a chief financial officer. Eric's old boss thought he could fill the bill nicely, and offered him the job. Eric accepted—quickly.

ERIC A. NELSON
143 Sixth Street, Indianola, Iowa 5001
Home: (515) 484-2679   Work: (515) 772-4839x253

PROFESSIONAL   Position in Cost/Financial Accounting leading to advanced
OBJECTIVE   managerial responsibilities.

EXPERIENCE   SAMPSON COMPANY, Des Moines, IA   11/88-Present
                Cost Accounting Supervisor
                * Supervise three-person staff.
                * Prepare month-end financial statement package.
                * Analyze financial and budget variances.
                * Advise upper-level management, engineering, sales and
                  production.
                * Recommend solutions for production to maintain standards.
                * Oversee financial performance.
                * Reconcile capital expenditures to fixed assets.
                * Audit current purchases to existing standards.
                * Maintain standard cost system, including evaluation of
                  bills of material and routing files.
                * Execute department supervisor responsibility for actual to
                  budget monthly performance analysis, including review of
                  potential highlights and detriments.
                * Revise and implement "work in process" system.

                FOSTER CORPORATION OF AMERICA, Osceola, IA 7/81-11/88
                Cost Accountant
                * Accomplished broad-based accounting functions, including
                  costing, financial statement preparation, payroll,
                  budgeting, accounts surveillance.
                * Developed/maintained costs for assigned product lines.
                * Evaluated product in direct relationship to engineering
                  labor and manufacturing costs, production/results control.
                * Controlled/evaluated ongoing audits of cycle counts and
                  reconciliation procedures related to inventory control.
                * Monitored problems related to product tracking;
                  implemented viable adjustments to cost projections.
                * Collaborated with other departments to coordinate cost
                  data and resolve cost problems (including planning,
                  purchasing, production engineering, design engineering,
                  operations, shop floor and marketing).

                ORCO INDUSTRIES INCORPORATED, Ames, IA 8/74-7/81
                Office Manager
                * Coordinated office operations for strip rubber
                  manufacturer.
                * Assumed bottom-line responsibility for all accounting
                  functions including financial statements, bank
                  reconciliations, payroll, accounts receivable/payable,
                  purchasing and commission determination.
                * Implemented standardized cost system, variance analysis
                  and budgeting.
                * Negotiated with suppliers and regional/national sales
                  representatives.
                * Spearheaded extensive credit/collections operations.
                * Supervised accounting and clerical staff.

WILLIAM J. RACK COMPANY, West Bend, IA   5/75-8/79
Traffic Manager/Lithographic Technician
* Coordinated all shipping/receiving transactions; evaluated
  orders.
* Supervised set-up and implemented various printing
  operations.

EDUCATION   IOWA STATE UNIVERSITY, Ames, IA   1982 - Present
             B.S., Accounting (expected 1996)
             3 years/99+ credits

             A.S., Accounting 1987

             IOWA WESLEYAN, Mt. Pleasant, IA   1979-1981
             Data processing/Accounting (19 credits)

INTERESTS   Active in West Bend Little League; sports enthusiast
             (softball, basketball, jogging); gardening

Index